Mr. Witt's Wid

A Frivolous Tale

Anthony Hope

Alpha Editions

This edition published in 2023

ISBN : 9789357954693

Design and Setting By
Alpha Editions
www.alphaedis.com
Email - info@alphaedis.com

Contents

CHAPTER I.
HOW GEORGE NESTON JUMPED.

THE Nestons, of Tottlebury Grange in the county of Suffolk, were an ancient and honourable family, never very distinguished or very rich, but yet for many generations back always richer and more distinguished than the common run of mankind. The men had been for the most part able and upright, tenacious of their claims, and mindful of their duties; the women had respected their betters, exacted respect from their inferiors, and educated their brothers' wives in the Neston ways; and the whole race, while confessing individual frailties, would have been puzzled to point out how, as a family, it had failed to live up to the position in which Providence and the Constitution had placed it. The error, if any, had indeed been on the other side in one or two cases. The last owner of the Grange, a gay old bachelor, had scorned the limits of his rents and his banking-account, and added victories on the turf to the family laurels at a heavy cost to the family revenues. His sudden death had been mourned as a personal loss, but silently acknowledged as a dynastic gain, and ten years of the methodical rule of his brother Roger had gone far to efface the ravages of his merry reign. The younger sons of the Nestons served the State or adorned the professions, and Roger had spent a long and useful life in the Office of Commerce. He had been a valuable official, and his merits had not gone unappreciated. Fame he had neither sought nor attained, and his name had come but little before the public, its rare appearances in the newspapers generally occurring on days when our Gracious Sovereign completed another year of her beneficent life, and was pleased to mark the occasion by conferring honour on Mr. Roger Neston. When this happened, all the leader-writers looked him up in "Men of the Time," or "Whitaker," or some other standard work of reference, and remarked that few appointments would meet with more universal public approval, a proposition which the public must be taken to have endorsed with tacit unanimity.

Mr. Neston went on his way, undisturbed by his moments of notoriety, but quietly pleased with his red ribbon, and, when he entered into possession of the family estate, continued to go to the office with unabated regularity. At last he reached the pinnacle of his particular ambition, and, as Permanent Head of his Department, for fifteen years took a large share in the government of a people almost unconscious of his existence, until the moment when it saw the announcement that on his retirement he had been raised to the peerage by the title of Baron Tottlebury. Then the chorus of approval broke forth once again, and the new lord had many friendly pats on the back he was turning to public life. Henceforth he sat silent in the House of Lords, and wrote letters to the *Times* on subjects which the cares of office had not previously left him leisure to study.

But fortune was not yet tired of smiling on the Nestons. Lord Tottlebury, before accepting his new dignity, had impressed upon his son Gerald the necessity of seeking the wherewith to gild the coronet by a judicious marriage. Gerald was by no means loth. He had never made much progress at the Bar, and felt that his want of success contrasted unfavourably with the growing practice of his cousin George, a state of things very unfitting, as George represented a younger branch than Gerald. A rich marriage, combined with his father's improved position, opened to him prospects of a career of public distinction, and, what was more important, of private leisure, better fitted to his tastes and less trying to his patience; and, by an unusual bit of luck, he was saved from any scruples about marrying for money by the fact that he was already desperately in love with a very rich woman. She was of no high birth, it is true, and she was the widow of a Manchester merchant; but this same merchant, to the disgust of his own relatives, had left her five thousand a year at her absolute disposal. The last fact easily outweighed the two first in Lord Tottlebury's mind, while Gerald rested his action on the sole ground that Neaera Witt was the prettiest girl in London, and, by Jove, he believed in the world; only, of course, if she had money too, all the better.

Accordingly, the engagement was an accomplished fact. Mrs. Witt had shown no more than a graceful disinclination to become Mrs. Neston. At twenty-five perpetual devotion to the memory of such a mere episode as her first marriage had been was neither to be desired nor expected, and Neaera was very frankly in love with Gerald Neston, a handsome, open-faced, strapping fellow, who won her heart mainly because he was so very unlike the late Mr. Witt. Everybody envied Gerald, and everybody congratulated Neaera on having escaped the various chasms that are supposed to yawn in the path of rich young widows. The engagement was announced once, and contradicted as premature, and then announced again; and, in a word, everything pursued its pleasant and accustomed course in these matters. Finally, Lord Tottlebury in due form entertained Mrs. Witt at dinner, by way of initiation into the Neston mysteries.

It was for this dinner that Mr. George Neston, barrister-at-law, was putting on his white tie one May evening in his chambers off Piccadilly. George was the son of Lord Tottlebury's younger brother. His father had died on service in India, leaving a wife, who survived him but a few years, and one small boy, who had developed into a rising lawyer of two or three-and-thirty, and was at this moment employed in thinking what a lucky dog Gerald was, if all people said about Mrs. Witt were true. Not that George envied his cousin his bride. His roving days were over. He had found what he wanted for himself, and Mrs. Witt's beauty, if she were beautiful, was nothing to him. So he thought with mingled joy and resignation. Still, however much you may be in love with somebody else, a pretty girl with five thousand a year is luck, and there's an end of it! So concluded George Neston as he got into his hansom, and drove to Portman Square.

The party was but small, for the Nestons were not one of those families that ramify into bewildering growths of cousins. Lord Tottlebury of course was there, a tall, spare, rather stern-looking man, and his daughter Maud, a bright and pretty girl of twenty, and Gerald, in a flutter ill concealed by the very extravagance of *nonchalance*. Then there were a couple of aunts and a male cousin and his wife, and George himself. Three of the guests were friends, not relatives. Mrs. Bourne had been the chosen intimate of Lord Tottlebury's dead wife, and he honoured his wife's memory by constant attention to her friend. Mrs. Bourne brought her daughter Isabel, and Isabel had come full of curiosity to see Mrs. Witt, and also hoping to see George Neston, for did she not know what pleasure it would give him to meet her? Lastly, there towered on the rug the huge form of Mr. Blodwell, Q.C., an old friend of Lord Tottlebury's and George's first tutor and kindly guide in the law, famous for rasping speeches in court and good stories out of it, famous, too, as one of the tallest men and quite the fattest man at the Bar. Only Neaera Witt was wanting, and before Mr. Blodwell had got well into the famous story about Baron Samuel and the dun cow Neaera Witt was announced.

Mrs. Witt's widowhood was only two years old, and she was at this time almost unknown to society. None of the party, except Gerald and his father, had seen her, and they all looked with interest to the door when the butler announced her name. She had put off her mourning altogether for the first time, and came in clothed in a gown of deep red, with a long train that gave her dignity, her golden hair massed low on her neck, and her pale, clear complexion just tinged with the suspicion of a blush as she instinctively glanced round for her lover. The entry was, no doubt, a small triumph. The girls were lost in generous admiration; the men were startled; and Mr. Blodwell, finishing the evening at the House of Commons, remarked to young Sidmouth Vane, the Lord President's private secretary (unpaid), "I hope, my boy, you may live as long as I have, and see as many pretty women; but you'll never see a prettier than Mrs. Witt. Her face! her hair! and Vane, my boy, her waist!" But here the division-bell rang, and Mr. Blodwell hastened off to vote against a proposal aimed at deteriorating, under the specious pretence of cheapening, the administration of justice.

Lord Tottlebury, advancing to meet Neaera, took her by the hand and proudly presented her to his guests. She greeted each gracefully and graciously until she came to George Neston. As she saw his solid jaw and clean-shaved keen face, a sudden light that looked like recollection leaped to her eyes, and her cheek flushed a little. The change was so distinct that

- 3 -

George was confirmed in the fancy he had had from the first moment she came in, that somewhere before he had seen that golden hair and those dark eyes, that combination of harmonious opposites that made her beauty no less special in kind than in degree. He advanced a step, his hand held half out, exclaiming—

"Surely——"

But there he stopped dead, and his hand fell to his side, for all signs of recognition had faded from Mrs. Witt's face, and she gave him only the same modestly gracious bow that she had bestowed on the rest of the party. The incident was over, leaving George sorely puzzled, and Lord Tottlebury a little startled. Gerald had seen nothing, having been employed in issuing orders for the march in to dinner.

The dinner was a success. Lord Tottlebury unbent; he was very cordial and, at moments, almost jovial. Gerald was in heaven, or at least sitting directly opposite and in full view of it. Mr. Blodwell enjoyed himself immensely: his classic stories had never yet won so pleasant a reward as Neaera's low rich laugh and dancing eyes. George ought to have enjoyed himself, for he was next to Isabel Bourne, and Isabel, heartily recognising that she was not to-night, as, to do her justice, she often was, the prettiest girl in the room, took the more pains to be kind and amusing. But George was ransacking the lumber-rooms of memory, or, to put it less figuratively, wondering, and growing exasperated as he wondered in vain, where the deuce he'd seen the girl before. Once or twice his eyes met hers, and it seemed to him that he had caught her casting an inquiring apprehensive glance at him. When she saw that he was looking, her expression changed into one of friendly interest, appropriate to the examination of a prospective kinsman.

"What do you think of her?" asked Isabel Bourne, in a low voice. "Beautiful, isn't she?"

"She is indeed," George answered, "I can't help thinking I've seen her somewhere before."

"She is a person one would remember, isn't she? Was it in Manchester?"

"I don't think so. I haven't been in Manchester more than two or three times in my life."

"Well, Maud says Mrs. Witt wasn't brought up there."

"Where was she brought up?"

"I don't know," said Isabel, "and I don't think Maud knew either. I asked Gerald, and he said she probably dropped down from heaven somewhere a few years ago."

"Perhaps that's how I come to remember her," suggested George.

Failing this explanation, he confessed himself puzzled, and determined to dismiss the matter from his thoughts for the present. Aided by Isabel Bourne, he was very successful in this effort: a pretty girl's company is the best modern substitute for the waters of Lethe.

Nevertheless, his interest remained strong enough to make him join the group which Gerald and Mr. Blodwell formed with Neaera as soon as the men went upstairs. Mr. Blodwell made no secret of the fact that it was with him a case of love at first sight, and openly regretted that his years prevented him fighting Gerald for his prize. Gerald listened with the complacent happiness of a secure lover, and Neaera gravely apologised for not having waited to make her choice till she had seen Mr. Blodwell.

"But at least you had heard of me?" he urged.

"I am terribly ignorant," she said. "I don't believe I ever did."

"Neaera's not one of the criminal classes, you see, sir," Gerald put in.

"He taunts me," exclaimed Mr. Blodwell, "with the Old Bailey!"

George had come up in time to hear the last two remarks. Neaera saw him, and smiled pleasantly.

"Here's a young lady who knows nothing about the law, George," continued Blodwell. "She never heard of me—nor of you either, I dare say. It reminds me of what they used to say about old Dawkins. Old Daw never had a brief, but he was Recorder of some little borough or other—place with a prisoner once in two years, you know—I forget the name. Let's see—yes, Peckton."

"Peckton!" exclaimed George Neston, loudly and abruptly.

Neaera made a sudden motion with one hand—a sudden motion suddenly checked—and her fan dropped with a clatter on the polished boards.

Gerald dived for it, so did Mr. Blodwell, and their heads came in contact with such violence as to drive all reminiscences of Recorder Dawkins out of Mr. Blodwell's brain. They were still indulging in recriminations, when Neaera swiftly left them, crossed to Lord Tottlebury, and took her leave.

George went to open the door for her. She looked at him curiously.

"Will you come and see me, Mr. Neston?" she asked.

He bowed gravely, answering nothing.

The party broke up, and as George was seeing Mr. Blodwell's bulk fitted into a four-wheeler, the old gentleman asked,

"Why did you do that, George?"

"What?"

"Jump, when I said Peckton."

"Oh, I used to go sessions there, you know."

"Do you always jump when people mention the places you used to go sessions at?"

"Generally," replied George.

"I see," said Mr. Blodwell, lighting his cigar. "A bad habit, George; it excites remark. Tell him the House."

"Good night, sir," said George. "I hope your head is better."

Mr. Blodwell snorted indignantly as he pulled up the window, and was driven away to his duties.

CHAPTER II.
WHY GEORGE NESTON JUMPED.

"HOW could I ever have forgotten?" said George, aloud, as he walked home. "I remember her now as if it was yesterday."

Memory, like much else that appertains to man, is a queer thing, and the name of Peckton had supplied the one link missing in his recollection. How, indeed, had he ever forgotten it? Can a man forget his first brief any more than his first love?—so like are they in their infinite promise, so like in their very finite results!

The picture was now complete in his mind: the little, muggy court at Peckton; old Dawkins, his wig black with age, the rest of him brown with snuff; the fussy clerk; the prosecuting counsel, son to the same fussy clerk; he himself, thrusting his first guinea into his pocket with shaking hand and beating heart (nervous before old Daw! Imagine!); the fat, peaceful policeman; the female warder, in her black straw-bonnet trimmed with dark-blue ribbons; and last of all, in the dock, a young girl, in shabby, nay, greasy, black, with pale cheeks, disordered hair, and swollen eyelids, gazing in blank terror on the majesty of the law, strangely expressed in the Recorder's ancient person. And, beyond all doubt or imagination of a doubt, the girl was Gerald's bride, Neaera Witt.

"I could swear to her to-day!" cried George.

She had scraped together a guinea for his fee. "I don't know where she got it from," the fat policeman said with professional cynicism as he gave it to George. "She pleads guilty and wants you to address the court." So George had, with infinite trepidation, addressed the court.

The girl had a father—drunk when not starving, and starving when not drunk. Now he was starving, and she had stolen the shoes (oh! the sordidness of it all!) to pawn, and buy food—or drink. It was a case for a caution merely—and—and—and George himself, being young to the work, stammered and stuttered as much from emotion as from fright. You see the girl was pretty!

All old Daw said was, "Do you know anything about her, policeman?" and the fat policeman said her father was a bad lot, and the girl did no work, and——

"That's enough," said old Daw; and, leaning forward, he pronounced his sentence:

"I'll deal lightly with you. Only"—shaking a snuffy forefinger—"take care you don't come here again! One calendar month, with hard labour."

And the girl, gazing back at honest old Daw, who would not have hurt a fly except from the Bench, softly murmured, "Cruel, cruel, cruel!" and was led away by the woman in the black straw bonnet.

Whereupon George did a very unprofessional thing. He gave his guinea, his firstborn son, back to the fat policeman, saying, "Give it her when she comes out. I can't take her money." At which the policeman smiled a smile that convicted George of terrible youthfulness.

It was all complete—all except the name by which the fussy clerk had called on the girl to plead, and which old Dawkins had mumbled out in sentencing her. That utterly escaped him. He was sure it was not "Neaera"—of course not "Neaera Witt;" but not "Neaera Anything," either. He would have remembered "Neaera."

"What on earth was it?" he asked himself as he unlocked his door and went upstairs. "Not that it matters much. Names are easily changed."

George Neston shared his chambers in Half Moon Street with the Honourable Thomas Buchanan Fillingham Myles, commonly known (as the peerage has it) as Tommy Myles. Tommy also had a small room in the Temple Chambers, where the two Nestons and Mr. Blodwell pursued their livelihood; but Tommy's appearances at the latter resort were few and brief. He did not trouble George much in Half Moon Street either, being a young man much given to society of all sorts, and very prone to be in bed when most people are up, and *vice versâ*. However, to-night he happened to be at home, and George found him with his feet on the mantelpiece, reading the evening paper.

"Well, what's she like?" asked Tommy.

"She's uncommonly pretty, and very pleasant," said George. Why say more, before his mind was made up?

"Who was she?" pursued Tommy, rising and filling his pipe.

"Ah! I don't know. I wish I did."

"Don't see that it matters to you. Anybody else there?"

"Oh, a few people."

"Miss Bourne?"

"Yes, she was there."

Tommy winked, sighed prodigiously, and took a large drink of brandy and soda.

"Where have you been?" asked George, changing the subject.

"Oh, to the Escurial—to a vulgar, really a very vulgar entertainment—as vulgar as you could find in London."

"Are you going out again?"

"My dear George! It's close on twelve!" said Tommy, in reproving tones.

"Or to bed?"

"No. George, you hurt my feelings. Can it be that you wish to be alone?"

"Well, at any rate, hold your tongue, Tommy. I want to think."

"Only one word. Has she been cruel?"

"Oh, get out. Here, give me a drink."

Tommy subsided into the *Bull's-eye*, that famous print whose motto is *Lux in tenebris* (meaning, of course, publicity in shady places), and George set himself to consider what he had best do in the matter of Neaera Witt.

The difficulties of the situation were obvious enough, but to George's mind they consisted not so much in the question of what to do as in that of how to do it. He had been tolerably clear from the first that Gerald must not marry Neaera without knowing what he could tell him; if he liked to do it afterwards, well and good. But of course he would not. No Neston would, thought George, who had his full share of the family pride. Men of good family made disgraceful marriages, it is true, but not with thieves; and anyhow nothing of the kind was recorded in the Neston annals. How should he look his uncle and Gerald in the face if he held his tongue? His course was very clear. Only—well, it was an uncommonly disagreeable part to be cast for— the denouncer and exposer of a woman who very probably was no worse than many another, and was unquestionably a great deal better-looking than most others. The whole position smacked unpleasantly of melodrama, and George must figure in the character of the villain, a villain with the best motives and the plainest duty. One hope only there was. Perhaps Mrs. Witt would see the wisdom of a timely withdrawal. Surely she would. She could never face the storm. Then Gerald need know nothing about it, and six months' travel—say to America, where pretty girls live—would bind up his broken heart. Only—again only—George did not much fancy the interview that lay before him. Mrs. Witt would probably cry, and he would feel a brute, and——

"Mr. Neston," announced Tommy's valet, opening the door.

Gerald had followed his cousin home, very anxious to be congratulated, and still more anxious not to appear anxious. Tommy received him with effusion. Why hadn't he been asked to the dinner? Might he call on Mrs. Witt? He heard she was a clipper; and so forth. George's felicitations stuck in his throat, but he got them out, hoping that Neaera would free him from the necessity of eating them up at some early date. Gerald was radiant. He seemed to have forgotten all about "Peckton," though he was loud in denouncing the unnatural hardness of Mr. Blodwell's head. Oh, and the last thing Neaera said was, would George go and see her?

"She took quite a fancy to you, old man," he said affectionately. "She said you reminded her of a judge."

George smiled. Was Neaera practising *double entente* on her betrothed?

"What an infernally unpleasant thing to say!" exclaimed Tommy.

"Of course I shall go and see her," said George,—"to-morrow, if I can find time."

"So shall I," added Tommy.

Gerald was pleased. He liked to see his taste endorsed with the approbation of his friends. "It's about time old George, here, followed suit, isn't it, Tommy? I've given him a lead."

George's attachment to Isabel Bourne was an accepted fact among his acquaintance. He never denied it: he did like her very much, and meant to marry her, if she would have him. And he did not really doubt that she would. If he had doubted, he would not have been so content to rest without an express assurance. As it was, there was no hurry. Let the practice grow a little more yet. He and Isabel understood one another, and, as soon as she was ready, he was ready. But long engagements were a nuisance to everybody. These were his feelings, and he considered himself, by virtue of them, to be in love with Isabel. There are many ways of being in love, and it would be a want of toleration to deny that George's is one of them, although it is certainly very unlike some of the others.

Tommy agreed that George was wasting his time, and with real kindness led Gerald back to the subject which filled his mind.

Gerald gladly embraced the opportunity. "Where did I meet her? Oh, down at Brighton, last winter. Then, you know, I pursued her to Manchester, and found her living in no end of a swell villa in the outskirts of that abominable place. Neaera hated it, but of course she had to live there while Witt was alive, and she had kept the house on."

"She wasn't Manchester-born, then?"

"No. I don't know where she was born. Her father seems to have been a romantic sort of old gentleman. He was a painter by trade—an artist, I mean, you know,—landscapes and so on."

"And went about looking for bits of nature to murder, eh?" asked Tommy.

"That's about it. I don't think he was any great shakes at it. At least, he didn't make much; and at last he settled in Manchester, and tried to pick up a living, working for the dealers. Witt was a picture-fancier, and, when Neaera came to sell, he saw her, and——"

"The late Witt's romance began?"

"Yes, confound him! I'm beastly jealous of old Witt, though he is dead."

"That's ungrateful," remarked George, "considering——"

"Hush! You'll wound his feelings," said Tommy. "He's forgotten all about the cash."

"It's all very well for you——" Gerald began.

But George cut in, "What was his name?"

"Witt's? Oh, Jeremiah, I believe."

"Witt? No. Hang Witt! The father's name."

"Oh!—Gale. A queer old boy he seems to have been—a bit of a scholar as well as an artist."

"That accounts for the 'Neaera,' I suppose," said Tommy.

"Neaera Gale," thought George. "I don't remember that."

"Pretty name, isn't it?" asked the infatuated Gerald.

"Oh, dry up!" exclaimed Tommy. "We can't indulge you any more. Go home to bed. You can dream about her, you know."

Gerald accepted this hint, and retired, still in that state of confident bliss that filled George's breast with trouble and dismay.

"I might as well be the serpent in Eden," he said, as he lay in bed, smoking dolefully.

CHAPTER III.
"WHAT ARE QUARTER-SESSIONS?"

THE atmosphere was stormy at No. 3, Indenture Buildings, Temple. It was four o'clock, and Mr. Blodwell had come out of court in the worst of bad tempers. He was savage with George Neston, who, being in a case with him, had gone away and left him with nobody to tell him his facts. He was savage with Tommy Myles, who had refused to read some papers for him; savage with Mr. Justice Pounce, who had cut up his speech to the jury,—Pounce, who had been his junior a hundred times!—savage with Mr. Timms, his clerk, because he was always savage with Timms when he was savage with other people. Tommy had fled before the storm; and now, to Mr. Blodwell's unbounded indignation, George also was brushing his hat with the manifest intention of departure.

"In my time, rising juniors," said Mr. Blodwell, with sarcasm, "didn't leave chambers at four."

"Business," said George, putting on his gloves.

"Women," answered his leader, briefly and scornfully.

"It's the same thing, in this case. I am going to see Mrs. Witt."

Mr. Blodwell's person expressed moral reprobation. George, however, remained unmoved, and the elder man stole a sharp glance at him.

"I don't know what's up, George," he said, "but take care of yourself."

"Nothing's up."

"Then why did you jump?"

"Timms, a hansom," cried George. "I'll be in court all day to-morrow, and keep you straight, sir."

"In Heaven's name, do. That fellow Pounce is such a beggar for dates. Now get out."

Mrs. Witt was living at Albert Mansions, the "swell villa" at Manchester having gone to join Mr. Witt in limbo. She was at home, and, as George entered, his only prayer was that he might not find Gerald in possession. He had no very clear idea how to proceed in his unpleasant task. "It must depend on how she takes it," he said. Gerald was not there, but Tommy Myles was, voluble, cheerful, and very much at home, telling Neaera stories of her lover's school-days. George chimed in as he best could, until Tommy rose to go, regretting the convention that drove one man to take his hat five minutes, at the latest, after another came in. Neaera pressed him to come again, but did not invite him to transgress the convention.

George almost hoped she would, for he was, as he confessed to himself, "funking it." There were no signs of any such feeling in Neaera, and no repetition of the appealing attitude she had seemed to take up the night before.

"She means to bluff me," thought George, as he watched her sit down in a low chair by the fire, and shade her face with a large fan.

"It is," she began, "so delightful to be welcomed by all Gerald's family and friends so heartily. I do not feel the least like a stranger."

"I came last night, hoping to join in that welcome," said George.

"Oh, I did not feel that you were a stranger at all. Gerald had told me so much about you."

George rose, and walked to the end of the little room and back. Then he stood looking down at his hostess. Neaera gazed pensively into the fire. It was uncommonly difficult, but what was the good of fencing?

"I saw you recognised me," he said, deliberately.

"In a minute. I had seen your photograph."

"Not only my photograph, but myself, Mrs. Witt."

"Have I?" asked Neaera. "How rude of me to forget! Where was it? Brighton?"

George's heart hardened a little. Of course she would lie, poor girl. He didn't mind that. But he did not like artistic lying, and Neaera's struck him as artistic.

"But are you sure?" she went on.

George decided to try a sudden attack. "Did they ever give you that guinea?" he said, straining his eyes to watch her face. Did she flush or not? He really couldn't say.

"I beg your pardon. Guinea?"

"Come, Mrs. Witt, we needn't make it more unpleasant than necessary. I saw you recognised me. The moment Mr. Blodwell spoke of Peckton I recognised you. Pray don't think I mean to be hard on you. I can and do make every allowance."

Neaera's face expressed blank astonishment. She rose, and made a step towards the bell. George was tickled. She had the amazing impertinence to convey, subtly but quite distinctly, by that motion and her whole bearing, that she thought he was drunk.

"Ring, if you like," he said, "or, rather, ask me, if you want the bell rung. But wouldn't it be better to settle the matter now? I don't want to trouble Gerald."

"I really believe you are threatening me with something," exclaimed Neaera. "Yes, by all means. Go on."

She motioned him to a chair, and stood above him, leaning one arm on the mantelpiece. She breathed a little quickly, but George drew no inference from that.

"Eight years ago," he said, slowly, "you employed me as your counsel. You were charged with theft—stealing a pair of shoes—at Peckton Quarter-Sessions. You retained me at a fee of one guinea."

Neaera was motionless, but a slight smile showed itself on her face. "What are Quarter-Sessions?" she asked.

"You pleaded guilty to the charge, and were sentenced to a month's imprisonment with hard labour. The guinea I asked you about was my fee. I gave it to that fat policeman to give back to you."

"Excuse me, Mr. Neston, but it's really too absurd." And Neaera relaxed her statuesque attitude, and laughed light-heartedly, deliciously. "No wonder you were startled last night—oh, yes, I saw that—if you identified your cousin's *fiancée* with this criminal you're talking about."

"I did and do identify her."

"Seriously?"

"Perfectly. It would be a poor joke."

"I never heard anything so monstrous. Do you really persist in it? I don't know what to say."

"Do you deny it?"

"Deny it! I might as well deny—but of course I deny it. It's madness."

"Then I must lay what I know before my uncle and Gerald, and leave them to act as they think best."

Neaera took a step forward as George rose from his seat. "Do you mean to repeat this atrocious—this insane scandal?"

"I think I must. I should be glad to think I had any alternative."

Neaera raised one white hand above her head, and brought it down through the air with a passionate gesture.

"I warn you not!" she cried; "I warn you not!"

George bowed.

"It is a lie, and—and if it were true, you could not prove it."

George thought this her first false step. But there were no witnesses.

"It will be war between us," she went on in growing excitement. "I will stand at nothing—nothing—to crush you; and I will do it."

"You must not try to frighten me," said George.

Neaera surveyed him from head to foot. Then she stretched out her white hand again, and said,

"Go!"

George shrugged his shoulders, took his hat, and went, feeling very much as if Neaera had detected him in theft. So great is the virtue of a good presence and dramatic instincts.

Suddenly he paused; then he went back again, and knocked at the door.

"Come in," cried Neaera.

As he entered she made an impatient movement. She was still standing where he had left her.

"Pray pardon me. I forgot to say one thing. Of course I am only interested in this—matter, as one of the family. I am not a detective. If you give up Gerald, my mouth is sealed."

"I will not give up Gerald," she exclaimed passionately. "I love him. I am not an adventuress; I am rich already. I——"

"Yes, you could look higher than Gerald, and avoid all this."

"I don't care. I love him."

George believed her. "I wish to God I could spare you——"

"Spare me? I don't ask your mercy. You are a slanderer——"

"I thought I would tell you," said George calmly.

"Will you not go?" she cried. And her voice broke into a sob.

This was worse than her tragedy airs. George fled without another word, cursing himself for a hard-hearted, self-righteous prig, and then cursing fate that laid this burden on him. What was she doing now, he wondered. Exulting in her triumph? He hoped so; for a different picture obstinately filled his mind—a beautiful woman, her face buried in her white arms, crying the brightness out of her eyes, all because George Neston had a sense of duty. Still he did not seriously waver in his determination. If Neaera had admitted the whole affair and besought his mercy, he felt that his resolution would have been sorely tried. But, as it was, he carried away the impression that he had to deal with a practised hand, and perhaps a little professional zeal mingled with his honest feeling that a woman who would lie like that was a woman who ought to be shown in her true colours.

"I'll tell uncle Roger and Gerald to-morrow," he thought. "Of course they will ask for proof. That means a journey to Peckton. Confound other people's affairs!"

George's surmise was right. Neaera Witt had spent the first half-hour after his departure in a manner fully as heart-rending as he had imagined. Everything was going so well. Gerald was so charming, and life looked, at last, so bright, and now came this! But Gerald was to dine with her, and there was not much time to waste in crying. She dried her eyes, and doctored them back into their lustre, and made a wonderful toilette. Then she entertained Gerald, and filled him with delight all a long evening. And at eleven o'clock, just as she was driving him out of his paradise, she said,

"Your cousin George was here to-day."

"Ah, was he? How did you get on with him?"

Neaera had brought her lover his hat. He needed a strong hint to move him. But she put the hat down, and knelt beside Gerald for a minute or two in silence.

"You look sad, darling," said he. "Did you and George quarrel?"

"Yes—I—— It's very dreadful."

"Why, what, my sweet?"

"No, I won't tell you now. He shan't say I got hold of you first, and prepossessed your mind."

"What in the world is wrong, Neaera?"

"You will hear, Gerald, soon. But you shall hear it from him. I will not—no, I will not be the first. But, Gerald dear, you will not believe anything against me?"

"Does George say anything against you?"

Neaera threw her arms round his neck. "Yes," she whispered.

"Then let him take care what it is. Neaera, tell me."

"No, no, no! He shall tell you first."

She was firm; and Gerald went away, a very mass of amazement and wrath.

But Neaera said to herself, when she was alone, "I think that was right. But, oh dear, oh dear! what a fuss about"—she paused, and added—"nothing!"

And even if it were not quite nothing, if it were even as much as a pair of shoes, the effect did threaten to be greatly out of proportion to the cause. Old Dawkins, and the fussy clerk, and the fat policeman could never have thought of such a coil as this, or surely, in defiance of all the laws of the land, they would have let that nameless damsel go.

CHAPTER IV.
A SERPENT IN EDEN.

ON mature reflection, Gerald Neston declined to be angry. At first, when he had heard George's tale, he had been moved to wrath, and had said bitter things about reckless talking, and even about malicious backbiting. But really, when you came to look at it, the thing was too absurd—not worth a moment's consideration—except that it had, of course, annoyed Neaera, and must, of course, leave some unpleasantness behind it. Poor old George! he had hunted up a mare's nest this time, and no mistake. No doubt he couldn't marry a thief; but who in his sober senses would attach any importance to this tale? George had done what he was pleased to think his duty. Let it rest. When he saw his folly, Neaera would forgive him, like the sweet girl she was. In fact, Gerald pooh-poohed the whole thing, and not the less because he had, not unnaturally, expected an accusation of quite another character, more unforgivable because not so outrageously improbable and wild.

Lord Tottlebury could not consent to treat what he described as "the incident" in quite so cavalier a fashion. He did not spare his hearers the well-worn precedent of Caesar's wife; and although, after an interview with Neaera, he was convinced of her innocence, it was in his opinion highly desirable that George should disabuse his own mind of this strange notion by some investigation.

"The marriage, in any case, will not take place for three months. Go and convince yourself of your mistake, and then, my dear George, we will make your peace with the lady. I need not caution you to let the matter go no further."

To be treated as a well-intentioned but misguided person is the most exasperating thing in the world, and George had hard work to keep his temper under the treatment. But he recognised that he might well have fared worse, and, in truth, he asked no more than a suspension of the marriage pending inquiry—a concession that he understood Lord Tottlebury was prepared to make, though proof must, of course, be forthcoming in reasonable time.

"I feel bound to look into it," he said. "As I have begun it, I will spare no pains. Nobody wishes more heartily than myself that I may have made an ass of myself." And he really did come as near to this laudable state of mind as it is in human nature to come.

Before the conference broke up, Lord Tottlebury suggested that there was one thing George could do at once—he could name the date of the trial at Peckton. George kept no diary, but he knew that the fateful expedition had been among his earliest professional journeys after his call to the Bar. Only very junior men went to Peckton, and, according to his recollection, the occurrence took place in the April following his call.

"April, eight years ago, was the time," he said. "I don't pledge myself to a day."

"You pledge yourself to the month?" asked his uncle.

"Yes, to the month, and I dare say I shall be able to find the day."

"And when will you go to Peckton?"

"Saturday. I can't possibly before."

The interview took place on the Tuesday evening, and on Wednesday Gerald went to lay the state of affairs before Neaera.

Neaera was petulant, scornful, almost flippant. More than all this, she was mysterious.

"Mr. George Neston has his reasons," she said. "He will not withdraw his accusation. I know he will not."

"My dearest, George is a first-rate fellow, as honourable as the day. If he finds—rather, when he finds——"

All Neaera said was, "Honourable!" But she put a great deal into that one word. "You dear, simple fellow!" she went on, "you have no suspicions of anybody. But let him take care how he persists."

More than this could not be got out of her, but she spoke freely about her own supposed misdoings, pouring a flood of ridicule and bitterness on George's unhappy head.

"A fool you call him!" she exclaimed, in reply to Gerald's half-hearted defence. "I don't know if he's a fool, but I hope he is no worse."

"Who's getting it so precious warm, Mrs. Witt?" inquired Tommy Myles's cheerful voice. "The door was ajar, and your words forced themselves—you know."

"How do you do, Mr. Myles?"

"As you'd invited me, and your servant wasn't about, the porter-fellow told me to walk up."

"I'm very glad you did. There's nothing you can't hear."

- 19 -

"Oh, I say, Neaera!" Gerald hastily exclaimed.

"Why shouldn't he hear?" demanded Neaera, turning on him in superb indignation. "Are you afraid that he'll believe it?"

"No; but we all thought——"

"I meant Mr. George Neston," said Neaera.

"George!" exclaimed Tommy.

"And I'll tell you why." And, in spite of Gerald's protest, she poured her tale of wrong into Tommy's sympathetic and wide-opened ears.

"There! Don't tell any one else. Lord Tottlebury says we mustn't. I don't mind, for myself, who knows it."

Tommy was overwhelmed. His mind refused to act. "He's a lunatic!" he declared. "I don't believe it's safe to live with him. He'll cut my throat, or something."

"Oh no; his lunacy is under control—a well-trained, obedient lunacy," said Neaera, relapsing into mystery.

"We all hope," said Gerald, "he'll soon find out his mistake, and nothing need come of it. Keep your mouth shut, my boy."

"All right. I'm silent as the cold tomb. But I'm da——"

"Have some more tea?" said Neaera, smiling very graciously. Should she not reward so warm a champion?

When the two young men took their leave and walked away together, Tommy vied even with Gerald in the loudness of his indignation.

"A lie! Of course it is, though I don't mean that old George don't believe it—the old ass! Why, the mere fact of her insisting on telling me about it is enough. She wouldn't do that if it's true."

"Of course not," assented Gerald.

"She'd be all for hushing it up."

Gerald agreed again.

"It's purely for George's sake we are so keen to keep it quiet," he added. "Though, of course, Neaera even wouldn't want it all over the town."

"I suppose I'd better tell George I know?"

"Oh yes. You'll be bound to show it in your manner."

George showed no astonishment at hearing that Neaera had made a confidant of Tommy Myles. It was quite consistent with the part she was playing, as he conceived it. Nor did he resent Tommy's outspoken rebukes.

"Don't mix yourself up in unpleasant things when you aren't obliged, my son," was all he said in reply to these tirades. "Dine at home?"

"No," snorted Tommy, in high dudgeon.

"You won't break bread with the likes of me?"

"I'm going to the play, and to supper afterwards."

"With whom?"

"Eunice Beauchamp."

"Dear me, what a pretty name!" said George. "Short for 'Betsy Jones,' I suppose?"

"Go to the devil," said Tommy. "You ain't going to accuse her of prigging, are you?"

"She kidnaps little boys," said George, who felt himself entitled to some revenge, "and keeps them till they're nearly grown up."

"I don't believe you ever saw her in your life."

"Oh yes, I did—first piece I ever went to, twenty years ago."

And so, what with Eunice Beauchamp, *alias* Betsy Jones, and Neaera Witt, *alias*—what?—two friends parted for that evening with some want of cordiality.

"She plays a bold game," thought George, as he ate his solitary chop; "but too bold. You overdo it, Mrs. Witt. An innocent girl would not tell that sort of thing to a stranger, however false it was."

Which reflection only showed that things strike different minds differently.

George needed comfort. The Serpent-in-Eden feeling was strong upon him. He wanted somebody who would not only recognise his integrity but also admire his discretion. He had a card for Mrs. Pocklington's at-home, and Isabel was to be there. He would go and have a talk with her; perhaps he would tell her all about it, for surely Neaera's confidence to Tommy Myles absolved him from the strict letter of his pledge of secrecy. Isabel was a sensible girl; she would understand his position, and not look on him as a cross between an idiot and a burglar because he had done what was obviously right. So George went to Mrs. Pocklington's with all the rest of the world; for everybody went there. Mrs. Pocklington—Eleanor Fitzderham, who married Pocklington, the great shipowner, member for Dockborough—had done more to unite the classes and the masses than hundreds of philanthropic societies, and, it may be added, in a pleasanter manner; and if, at her parties, the bigwigs did not always talk to the littlewigs, yet the littlewigs were in the same room with the bigwigs, which is something even at the moment, and really very nearly as good for purposes of future reference.

George made his way across the crowded rooms, recognising many acquaintances as he went. There was Mr. Blodwell talking to the last new beauty—he had a wonderful knack of it,—and Sidmouth Vane talking to the last new heiress, who would refuse him in a month or two. An atheistic philosopher was discussing the stagnation of the stock-markets with a high-church Bishop—Mrs. Pocklington always aimed at starting people on their points of common interest: and Lady Wheedleton, of the Primrose League, was listening to Professor Dressingham's description of the newest recipe for manure, with an impression that the subject was not quite decent, but might be useful at elections. General Sir Thomas Swears was asking if anybody had seen the Secretary for War—he had a word to say to him about the last rifle; but nobody had. The Countess Hilda von Someveretheim was explaining the problem of "Darkest England" to the Minister of the Republic of Compostella; Judge Cutter, the American mystic, was asking the captain of the Oxford Boat Club about the philosophy of Hegel, and Miss Zoe Ballance, the pretty actress, was discussing the relations of art and morality with Colonel Belamour of the Guards.

George was inclined to resent the air of general enjoyment that pervaded the place: it seemed a little unfeeling. But he was comforted by catching sight of Isabel. She was talking to a slight young man who wore an eye-glass and indulged in an expression of countenance which invited the conclusion that he was overworked and overstrained. Indeed, he was just explaining to Miss Bourne that it was not so much long hours as what he graphically described as the "tug on his nerves" that wore him out. Isabel had never suffered from this particular torture, but she was very sympathetic, said that she had often heard the same from other literary men (which was true), and promised to go down to supper with Mr. Espion later in the evening. Mr. Espion went about his business (for, the fact is, he was "doing" the party for the *Bull's-eye*), and the coast was left clear for George, who came up with a deliberately lugubrious air. Of course Isabel asked him what was the matter; and, somehow or other, it happened that in less than ten minutes she was in possession of all the material facts, if they were facts, concerning Neaera Witt and the pair of shoes.

The effect was distinctly disappointing. Amiability degenerates into simplicity when it leads to the refusal to accept obvious facts merely because they impugn the character of an acquaintance; and what is the use of feminine devotion if it boggles over accepting what you say, just because you say something a little surprising? George was much annoyed.

"I am not mistaken," he said. "I did not speak hastily."

"Of course not," said Isabel. "But—but you have no actual proof, have you, George?"

"Not yet; but I soon shall have."

"Well, unless you get it very soon——"

"Yes?"

"I think you ought to withdraw what you have said, and apologise to Mrs. Witt."

"In fact, you think I was wrong to speak at all?"

"I think I should have waited till I had proof; and then, perhaps——"

"Everybody seems to think me an ass."

"Not *that*, George; but a little—well—reckless."

"I shan't withdraw it."

"Not if you get no proof?"

George shirked this pointed question, and, as the interview was really less soothing than he had expected, took an early opportunity of escaping.

Mr. Espion came back, and asked why Neston had gone away looking so sulky. Isabel smiled and said Mr. Neston was vexed with her. Could anybody be vexed with Miss Bourne? asked Mr. Espion, and added,

"But Neston is rather crotchety, isn't he?"

"Why do you say that?" asked Isabel.

"Oh, I don't know. Well, the fact is, I was talking to Tommy Myles at the Cancan——"

"Where, Mr. Espion?"

"At the theatre, and he told me Neston had got some maggot in his head——"

"I don't think he ought to say that."

But need we listen longer? And whose fault was it—Neaera's, or George's, or Isabel's, or Tommy's, or Mr. Espion's? That became the question afterwards, when Lord Tottlebury was face to face with the violated compact,—and with next day's issue of the *Bull's-eye*.

CHAPTER V.
THE FIRST PARAGRAPH—AND OTHERS.

UNDER pressure of circumstances men very often do what they have declared they cannot possibly do; it happens with private individuals no less than with political parties. George declared he could not possibly go to Peckton before Saturday; but he was so disgusted with his position, that he threw all other engagements to the winds, and started early on Thursday morning, determined not to face his friends again without attempting to prove his words. Old Dawkins was dead, but the clerk was, and the policeman might be, alive; and, on his return to town, he could see Jennings, the clerk's son, who had settled down to conveyancing in Lincoln's Inn, and try to refresh his memory with materials gathered on the spot. For George had already seen Mr. Jennings, and Mr. Jennings remembered nothing about it—it was not his first brief,—but was willing to try to recall the matter if George would get him the details and let him see a picture of the person wanted—a request George did not wish to comply with at the moment.

So he went to Peckton, and found out perhaps as much as he could reasonably expect to find out, as shall in due course appear. And during his absence several things happened. In the first place, the *Bull's-eye* was published, containing what became known as the "First Paragraph." The "First Paragraph" was headed "Strange Charge against a Lady—Rumoured Proceedings," and indicated the Neston family, Neaera Witt, and George, in such a manner as to enable their friends to identify them. This paragraph was inserted with the object of giving Neaera, or George, or both of them, as the case might be, or anybody else who could be "drawn," an opportunity of contradicting it. The second event was that the Nestons' friends did identify them, and proceeded to open the minds of everybody who did not.

Then Mr. Blodwell read the *Bull's-eye*, as his custom was, and thoughtfully ejaculated "Peckton!" and Lord Tottlebury, being at the club, was shown the *Bull's-eye* by a friend, who really could not do less, and went home distracted; and Tommy Myles read it, and, conscience-stricken, fled to Brighton for three days' fresh air; and Isabel read it, and confessed to her mother, and was scolded, and cried; and Gerald read it, and made up his mind to kick everybody concerned, except, of course, Neaera; and, finally, Neaera read it, and was rather frightened and rather excited, and girt on her armour for battle.

Gerald, however, was conscious that the process he had in his mind, satisfying as it would be to his own feelings, would not prove in all respects a solution of the difficulty, and, with the selfishness which a crisis in a man's own affairs engenders, he made no scruple about taking up a full hour of Mr. Blodwell's time, and expounding his views at great length, under the guise of taking counsel. Mr. Blodwell listened to his narrative of facts with interest, but cut short his stream of indignant comment.

"The mischief is that it's got into the papers," he said. "But for that, I don't see that it matters much."

"Not matter much?" gasped Gerald.

"I suppose you don't care whether it's true or not?"

"It's life or death to me," answered Gerald.

"Bosh! She won't steal any more shoes now she's a rich woman."

"You speak, sir, as if you thought——"

"Haven't any opinion on the subject, and it wouldn't be of any importance if I had. The question is shortly this: Supposing it to be true, would you marry her?"

Gerald flung himself into a chair, and bit his finger nail.

"Eight years is a long while ago; and poverty's a hard thing; and she's a pretty girl."

"It's an absurd hypothesis," said Gerald. "But a thief's a thief."

"True. So are a good many other people."

"I should have to consider my father and—and the family."

"Should you? I should see the family damned. However, it comes to this— if it were true, you wouldn't marry her."

"How could I?" groaned Gerald. "We should be cut."

Mr. Blodwell smiled.

"Well, my ardent lover," he said, "that being so, you'd better do nothing till you see whether it's true."

"Not at all. I only took the hypothesis; but I haven't the least doubt that it's a lie."

"A mistake—yes. But it's in the *Bull's-eye*, and a mistake in the newspapers needs to be reckoned with."

"What shall I do?"

"Wait till George comes back. Meanwhile, hold your tongue."

"I shall contradict that lie."

"Much better not. Don't write to them, or see them, or let anybody else till George comes back. And, Gerald, if I were you, I shouldn't quarrel with George."

"He shall withdraw it, or prove it."

Mr. Blodwell shrugged his shoulders and became ostentatiously busy with the case of *Pigg* v. *the Local Board of Slushton-under-Mudd*. "A very queer point this," he remarked. "The drainage system of Slushton is——" And he stopped with a chuckle at the sight of Gerald's vanishing back. He called after him—

"Are you going to Mrs. Witt's this afternoon?"

"No," answered Gerald. "This evening."

Mr. Blodwell sat at work for ten minutes more. Then he rang the bell.

"Mr. Neston gone, Timms?"

"Yes, sir."

"Then get a four-wheeler." And he added to himself, "I should like to see her again, under this new light. I wonder if she'll let me in."

Neaera did let him in. In fact, she seemed very glad to see him, and accepted with meekness her share of his general censure on the "babbling" that had gone on.

"You see," she said, handing him a cup of tea, "it scarcely seemed a serious matter to me. I was angry, of course, but almost more amused than angry."

"Naturally," answered Mr. Blodwell. "But, my dear young lady, everything which is public is serious. And this thing is now public, for no doubt to-morrow's *Bull's-eye* will give all your names and addresses."

"I don't care," said Neaera.

Mr. Blodwell shook his head. "You must consider Gerald and his people."

"Gerald doesn't doubt me. If he did——" Neaera left her recreant lover's fate to the imagination.

"But Lord Tottlebury and the world at large? The world at large always doubts one."

"I suppose so," said Neaera, sadly. "Fortunately, I have conclusive proof."

"My dear Mrs. Witt, why didn't you say so before?"

"Before there was anything to meet? Is that your way, Mr. Blodwell?"

"George may bring back something to meet."

Neaera rose and went to her writing-table. "I don't know why I shouldn't show it to you," she said. "I was just going to send it to Lord Tottlebury. It will be a pleasant surprise for Mr. George Neston when he comes back from Peckton with his proofs!" She handed Mr. Blodwell a sheet of note-paper.

He took it, throwing one quick glance at Neaera. "You wish me to read this?"

"It's letting you into the secrets of my early days," she said. "You see, I wasn't always as well off as I am now."

Mr. Blodwell adjusted his eye-glass and perused the document, which set forth that Miss N. Gale entered the service of Mrs. Philip Horne, of Balmoral Villa, Bournemouth, as companion to that lady, in March, 1883, and remained in such service until the month of July, 1883; that, during the whole of such period, she conducted herself with propriety; that she read aloud with skill, ordered a household with discretion, and humoured a fussy old lady with tact (this is a paraphrase of the words of the writer); finally, that she left, by her own desire, to the regret of the above-mentioned Susan Horne.

Neaera watched Mr. Blodwell as he read.

"Eighteen eighty-three?" said he; "that's the year in question?"

"Yes, and April is the month in question—the month I am supposed to have spent in prison!"

"You didn't show this to George?"

"No. Why should I? Besides, I didn't know then when he dated my crime."

Mr. Blodwell thought it a little queer that she had not asked him. "He should certainly see it at once. Have you seen anything of Mrs. Horne lately?"

"Oh no; I should be afraid she must be dead. She was an old lady, and very feeble."

"It is—it may be—very lucky—your having this."

"Yes, isn't it? I should never have remembered the exact time I went to Mrs. Horne's."

Mr. Blodwell took his departure in a state of mind that he felt was unreasonable. Neaera had been, he told himself, most frank, most charming, most satisfactory. Yet he was possessed with an overpowering desire to cross-examine Neaera.

"Perhaps it's only habit," he said to himself. "A protestation of innocence raises all my fighting instincts."

The next day witnessed the publication of the "Second Paragraph," and the second paragraph made it plain to everybody that somebody must vindicate his or her character. The public did not care who did it, but it felt itself entitled to an action, wherein the whole matter should be threshed out for the furtherance of public justice and entertainment. The *Bull's-eye* itself took this view. It implored Neaera, or George, or somebody to sue it, if they would not sue one another. It had given names, addresses, dates, and details. Could the most exacting plaintiff ask more? If no action were brought, it was clear that Neaera had stolen the shoes, and that George had slandered her, and that the Nestons in general shrank from investigation into the family history; all this was still clearer, if they pursued their extraordinary conduct in not forwarding personal narratives for the information of the public and the accommodation of the *Bull's-eye*.

Into this turmoil George was plunged on his return from Peckton. He had been detained there two days, and did not reach his rooms till late on Friday evening. He was greeted by two numbers of the *Bull's-eye*, neatly displayed on his table; by a fiery epistle from Gerald, demanding blood or apologies; by two penitential dirges from Isabel Bourne and Tommy Myles; and, lastly, by a frigid note from Lord Tottlebury, enclosing the testimony of Mrs. Philip Horne to the character and accomplishments of Miss N. Gale. In Lord Tottlebury's opinion, only one course was, under the circumstances, open to a gentleman.

Philanthropists often remark, *à propos* of other philanthropists, that it is easier to do harm than good, even when you are, as it were, an expert in doing good. George began to think that his amateur effort at preserving the family reputation and punishing a wrongdoer looked like vindicating the truth of this general principle. Here was a hornets'-nest about his ears! And would what he brought back with him make the buzzing less furious or the stings less active? He thought not.

"Can a girl be in two places at once," he asked,—"in one of her Majesty's prisons, and also at—where is it?—Balmoral Villa, Bournemouth?" And he laid side by side Mrs. Horne's letter and a certain photograph which was among the spoils of his expedition.

George had not the least doubt that it was a photograph of Neaera Witt, for all that it was distinctly inscribed, "Nelly Game." Beyond all question it was a photograph of the girl who stole the shoes, thoughtfully taken and preserved with a view to protecting society against future depredations at her hands. It was Crown property, George supposed, and probably he had no business with it, but a man can get many things he has no business with for half a sovereign, the sum George had paid for the loan of it. It must be carefully remembered that Peckton is exceptional, not typical, in the laxity of its administration, and a long reign of solitary despotism had sapped the morality of the fat policeman.

The art of photography has made much progress in recent years. It is less an engine for the reduction of self-conceit than it used to be, and less a means of revealing how ill-looking a given person can appear under favourable circumstances. But Peckton was behind the time, here as everywhere. Nelly Game's portrait did faint justice to Neaera Witt, and eight years' wear had left it blurred and faded almost to the point of indistinctness. It was all very well for George to recognise it. In candour he was bound to admit that he doubted if it would convince the unwilling. Besides, a great change comes between seventeen and five-and-twenty, even when Seventeen is not half-starved and clad in rags, Five-and-twenty living in luxury, and decked in the glories of millinery.

"It won't do alone," he said, "but it will help. Let's have a look at this—document." When he had read it he whistled gently. "Oh, ho! an alibi. Now I've got her!" he exclaimed.

But had he? He carefully re-read the letter. It was a plausible enough letter, and conclusive, unless he was prepared to charge Mrs. Witt with deeper schemes and more dangerous accomplishments than he had yet thought of doing.

Men are mistaken sometimes, said a voice within him; but he would not listen.

"I'll look at that again to-morrow," he said, "and find out who 'Susan Horne' is."

Then he read his letters, and cursed his luck, and went to bed a miserable man.

The presentment of truth, not the inculcation of morality, being the end of art, it is worth while to remark that he went to bed a miserable man simply and solely because he had tried to do his duty.

CHAPTER VI.
A SUCCESSFUL ORDEAL.

THE general opinion was that Gerald Neston behaved foolishly in allowing himself to be interviewed by the *Bull's-eye*. Indeed, it is rather odd, when we consider the almost universal disapproval of the practice of interviewing, to see how frequent interviews are. *Damnantur et crescunt*; and mankind agrees to excuse its own weakness by postulating irresistible ingenuity and audacity in the interviewer. So Gerald was publicly blamed and privately blessed for telling the *Bull's-eye* that an atrocious accusation had been brought against the lady referred to, and brought by one who should have been the last to bring it, and would, he hoped, be the first to withdraw it. The accusation did seriously concern the lady's character, and nothing but the fullest apology could be accepted. He preferred not to go into details at present; indeed, he hoped it would never be necessary to do so.

Such might be Gerald's hope. It was not the hope of the *Bull's-eye*, nor, indeed, of society in general. What could be more ill-advised than to hint dreadful things and refuse full information? Such a course simply left the imagination to wander, fancy free, through the Newgate Calendar, attributing to Mrs. Witt—the name of the slandered lady was by this time public property—all or any of the actions therein recorded.

"It's like a blank bill," said Charters, the commercial lawyer, to Mr. Blodwell; "you fill it up for as much as the stamp will cover."

"The more gossiping fool you," replied Mr. Blodwell, very rudely, and quite unjustifiably, for the poor man merely meant to indicate a natural tendency, not to declare his own idea of what was proper. But Mr. Blodwell was cross; everybody had made fools of themselves, he thought, and he was hanged— at least hanged—if he saw his way out of it.

George's name had not as yet been actually mentioned, but everybody knew who it was,—that "relative of Lord Tottlebury, whose legal experience, if nothing else, should have kept him from bringing ungrounded accusations;" and George's position was far from pleasant. He began to see, or fancy he saw, men looking askance at him; his entrance was the occasion of a sudden pause in conversation; his relations with his family were, it need hardly be said, intolerable to the last degree; and, finally, Isabel Bourne had openly gone over to the enemy, had made her mother invite Neaera Witt to dinner, and had passed George in the park with the merest mockery of a bow. He was anxious to bring matters to an issue one way or another, and with this end he wrote to Lord Tottlebury, asking him to arrange a meeting with Mrs. Witt.

"As you are aware," he said, "I have been to Peckton. I have already told you what I found there, so far as it bore on the fact of 'Nelly Game's' conviction. I now desire to give certain persons who were acquainted with 'Nelly Game' an opportunity of seeing Mrs. Witt. No doubt she will raise no objections. Blodwell is willing to put his chambers at our disposal; and I think this would be the best place, as it will avoid the gossip and curiosity of the servants. Will Mrs. Witt name a day and time? I and my companions will make a point of suiting her convenience."

George's "companions" were none other than the fussy clerk and the fat policeman. The female warder had vanished; and although there were some prison officials whose office dated from before Nelly Game's imprisonment, George felt that, unless his first two witnesses were favourable, it would be useless to press the matter, and did not at present enlist their services. Mr. Jennings, the Lincoln's Inn barrister, had proved utterly hopeless. George showed him the photograph. "I shouldn't have recognized it from Eve's," said Mr. Jennings; and George felt that he might, without duplicity, ignore such a useless witness.

Neaera laughed a little at the proposal when it was submitted to her, but expressed her willingness to consent to it. Gerald was almost angry with her for not being angry at the indignity.

"He goes too far: upon my word he does;" he muttered.

"What does it matter, dear?" asked Neaera. "It will be rather fun."

Lord Tottlebury raised a hand in grave protest.

"My dear Neaera!" said he.

"Not much fun for George," Gerald remarked in grim triumph.

"I suppose Mr. Blodwell's chambers will do?" asked Lord Tottlebury. "It seems convenient."

But here Neaera, rather to his surprise, had her own views. She wasn't going down to musty chambers to be stared at—yes, Gerald, all lawyers stared,—and taken for a breach-of-promise person, and generally besmirched with legal mire. No: nor she wouldn't have Mr. George Neston's spies in her house; nor would she put herself out the least about it.

"Then it must be in my house," said Lord Tottlebury.

Neaera acquiesced, merely adding that the valuables had better be locked up.

"And when? We had better say some afternoon, I suppose."

"I am engaged every afternoon for a fortnight."

"My dear," said Lord Tottlebury, "business must take precedence."

Neaera did not see it; but at last she made a suggestion. "I am dining with you *en famille* the day after to-morrow. Let them come then."

"That'll do," said George. "Ten minutes after dinner will settle the whole business."

Lord Tottlebury made no objection. George had suggested that a couple of other ladies should be present, to make the trial fairer; and it was decided to invite Isabel Bourne, and Miss Laura Pocklington, daughter of the great Mrs. Pocklington. Mrs. Pocklington would come with her daughter, and it was felt that her presence would add authority to the proceedings. Maud Neston was away; indeed, her absence had been thought desirable, pending the settlement of this unpleasant affair.

Lord Tottlebury always made the most of his chances of solemnity, and, if left to his own bent, would have invested the present occasion with an impressiveness not far short of a death sentence. But he was powerless in face of the determined frivolity with which Neaera treated the whole matter. Mrs. Pocklington found herself, apparently, invited to assist at a farce, instead of a melodrama, and with her famous tact at once recognised the situation, her elaborate playfulness sanctioned the hair-brained chatter of the girls, and made Gerald's fierce indignation seem disproportionate to the subject. Dinner passed in a whirl of jokes and gibes, George affording ample material; and afterwards the ladies, flushed with past laughter, and constantly yielding to fresh hilarity at Neaera's sallies, awaited the coming of George and his party with no diminution of gaiety.

A knock was heard at the door.

"Here are the minions of the law, Mrs. Witt!" cried Laura Pocklington.

"Then I must prepare for the dungeon," said Neaera, and rearranged her hair before a mirror.

"It quite reminds me," said Mrs. Pocklington, "of the dear Queen of Scots."

Lord Tottlebury was, in spite of his preoccupations, beginning to argue about the propriety of Mrs. Pocklington's epithet, when George was shown in. He looked weary, bored, disgusted. After shaking hands with Lord Tottlebury, he bowed generally to the room, and said,

"I propose to bring Mr. Jennings, the clerk, in first; then the policeman. It will be better they should come separately."

Lord Tottlebury nodded. Gerald had ostentatiously turned his back on his cousin. Mrs. Pocklington fanned herself with an air of amused protest, which the girls reproduced in a broader form. No one spoke, till Neaera herself said with a laugh,

"Arrange your effects as you please, Mr. Neston."

George looked at her. She was dressed with extraordinary richness, considering the occasion. Her neck and arms, disclosed by her evening gown, glittered with diamonds; a circlet of the same stones adorned her golden hair, which was arranged in a lofty erection on her head. She met his look with derisive defiance, smiling in response to the sarcastic smile on his face. George's smile was called forth by the recognition of his opponent's tactics. Her choice of time and place had enabled her to call to her aid all the arts of millinery and the resources of wealth to dazzle and blind the eyes of those who sought to find in her the shabby draggle-tailed girl of eight years before. Old Mr. Jennings had come under strong protest. He was, he said, half blind eight years ago, and more than half now; he had seen hundreds of interesting young criminals and could no more recognise one from another than to-day's breakfast egg from yesterday week's; as for police photographs, everybody knew they only darkened truth. Still he came, because George had constrained him.

Neaera, Isabel, and Laura Pocklington took their places side by side, Neaera on the right, leaning her arm on the chimney-piece, in her favourite pose of languid haughtiness; Isabel was next her. Lord Tottlebury met Mr. Jennings with cold civility, and gave him a chair. The old man wiped his spectacles and put them on. A pause ensued.

"George," said Lord Tottlebury, "I suppose you have explained?"

"Yes," said George. "Mr. Jennings, can you say whether any, and which, of the persons present is Nelly Game?"

Gerald turned round to watch the trial.

"Is the person suspected—supposed to be Nelly Game—in the room?" asked Mr. Jennings, with some surprise. He had expected to see a group of maid-servants.

"Certainly," said Lord Tottlebury, with a grim smile. And Mrs. Pocklington chuckled.

"Then I certainly can't," said Mr. Jennings. And there was an end of that, an end no other than what George had expected. The fat policeman was his sheet-anchor.

The fat policeman, or to give him his proper name, Sergeant Stubbs, unlike Mr. Jennings, was enjoying himself. A trip to London *gratis*, with expenses on a liberal scale, and an identification at the end—could the heart of mortal constable desire more? Know the girl? Of course he would, among a thousand! It was his business to know people and he did not mean to fail, especially in the service of so considerate an employer. So he walked in confidently, sat himself down, and received his instructions with professional imperturbability.

The ladies stood and smiled at Stubbs. Stubbs sat and peered at the ladies, and, being a man at heart, thought they were a set of as likely girls as he'd ever seen; so he told Mrs. Stubbs afterwards. But which was Nelly Game?

"It isn't her in the middle," said Stubbs, at last.

"Then," said George, "we needn't trouble Miss Bourne any longer."

Isabel went and sat down, with a scornful toss of her head, and Laura Pocklington and Neaera stood side by side.

"I feel as if it were the judgment of Paris," whispered the latter, audibly, and Mrs. Pocklington and Gerald tittered. Stubbs had once been to Paris on business, but he did not see what it had to do with the present occasion, unless indeed it were something about a previous conviction.

"It isn't her," he said, after another pause, pointing a stumpy forefinger at Laura Pocklington.

There was a little shiver of dismay. George rigidly repressed every indication of satisfaction. Neaera stood calm and smiling, bending a look of amused kindliness on Stubbs; but the palm of the white hand on the mantelpiece grew pink as the white fingers pressed against it.

"Would you like to see me a little nearer?" she asked, and, stepping forward to where Stubbs sat, she stood right in front of him.

George felt inclined to cry "Brava!" as if he were at the play.

Stubbs was puzzled. There was a likeness, but there was so much unlikeness too. It really wasn't fair to dress people up differently. How was a man to know them?

"Might I see the photograph again, sir?" he asked George.

"Certainly not," exclaimed Gerald, angrily.

George ignored him.

"I had rather," he said, "you told us what you think without it."

George had sent Lord Tottlebury the photograph, and everybody had looked at it and declared it was not the least like Neaera.

Stubbs resumed his survey. At last he said, pressing his hand over his eyes,

"I can't swear to her, sir."

"Very well," said George. "That'll do."

But Neaera laughed.

"Swear to me, Mr. Stubbs!" said she. "But do you mean you think I'm like this Nelly Games?"

"'Game,' not 'Games,' Mrs. Witt," said George, smiling again.

"Well, then, 'Game.'"

"Yes, miss, you've a look of her."

"Of course she has," said Mrs. Pocklington, "or Mr. George would never have made the mistake." Mrs. Pocklington liked George, and wanted to let him down easily.

"That's all you can say?" asked Lord Tottlebury.

"Yes, sir; I mean, my lord."

"It comes to nothing," said Lord Tottlebury, decisively.

"Nothing at all," said George. "Thank you, Stubbs. I'll join you and Mr. Jennings in a moment."

"Good-bye, Mr. Stubbs," said Neaera. "I'm sure I should have known you if I'd ever seen you before."

Stubbs withdrew, believing himself to have received a compliment.

"Of course this ends the matter, George," said Lord Tottlebury.

"I should hope so," said Gerald.

George looked at Neaera; and as he looked the conviction grew stronger on him that she was Nelly Game.

"Mr. George Neston is not convinced," said she, mockingly.

"It does not much matter whether I am convinced or not," said George. "There is no kind of evidence to prove the identity."

Gerald sprang up in indignation. "Do you mean that you won't retract?"

"You can state all the facts; I shall say nothing."

"You shall apologise, or——"

"Gerald," said Lord Tottlebury, "this is no use."

There was a feeling that George was behaving very badly. Everybody thought so, and said so; and all except Neaera either exhorted or besought him to confess himself the victim of an absurd mistake. As the matter had become public, nothing less could be accepted.

George wavered. "I will let you know to-morrow," he said. "Meanwhile let me return this document to Mrs. Witt." He took out Mrs. Horne's letter and laid it on the table. "I have ventured to take a copy," he said. "As the original is valuable, I thought I had better give it back."

"Thank you," said Neaera, and moved forward to take it.

Gerald hastened to fetch it for her. As he took it up, his eye fell on the writing, for George had laid it open on the table.

"Why, Neaera," said he, "it's in your handwriting!"

George started, and he thought he saw Neaera start just perceptibly.

"Of course," she said. "That's only a copy."

"My dear, you never told me so," said Lord Tottlebury; "and I have never seen your handwriting."

"Gerald and Maud have."

"But they never saw this."

"It was stupid of me," said Neaera, penitently; "but I never thought of there being any mistake. What difference does it make?"

George's heart was hardened. He was sure she had, if not tried to pass off the copy as an original from the first, at any rate taken advantage of the error.

"Have you the original?" he asked.

"No," said Neaera. "I sent it to somebody ever so long ago, and never got it back."

"When did you make this copy?"

"When I sent away the original."

"To whom?" began George again.

"I won't have it," cried Gerald. "You shan't cross-examine her with your infernal insinuations. Do you mean that she forged this?"

George grew stubborn.

"I should like to see the original," he said.

"Then you can't," retorted Gerald, angrily.

George shrugged his shoulders, turned, and left the room.

And they all comforted and cosseted Neaera, and abused George, and made up their minds to let the world know how badly he was behaving.

"It's our duty to society," said Lord Tottlebury.

CHAPTER VII.
AN IMPOSSIBLE BARGAIN.

"I SHOULD eat humble-pie, George," said Mr. Blodwell, tapping his eye-glasses against his front teeth. "She's one too many for you."

"Do you think I'm wrong?"

"On the whole, I incline to think you're right. But I should eat humble-pie if I were you, all the same."

The suggested diet is palatable to nobody, and the power of consuming it without contortion is rightly put high in the list of virtues, if virtue be proportionate to difficulty. To a man of George Neston's temperament penance was hard, even when enforced by the consciousness of sin; to bend the knees in abasement, when the soul was erect in self-approval, came nigh impossibility.

Still it was unquestionably necessary that he should assume the sheet and candle, or put up with an alternative hardly, if at all, less unpleasant. The "Fourth Paragraph" had appeared. It was called a paragraph for the sake of uniformity, but it was in reality a narrative, stretching to a couple of columns, and giving a detailed account of the attempted identification. For once, George implicitly believed the editor's statement that his information came to him on unimpeachable authority. The story was clearly not only inspired by, but actually written by the hand of Gerald himself, and it breathed a bitter hostility to himself that grieved George none the less because it was very natural. This hostility showed itself, here and there, in direct attack; more constantly in irony and ingenious ridicule. George's look, manner, tones, and walk were all pressed into the service. In a word, the article certainly made him look an idiot; he rather thought it made him look a malignant idiot.

"What can you do?" demanded Mr. Blodwell again. "You can't bring up any more people from Peckton. You chose your witnesses, and they let you in."

George nodded.

"You went to Bournemouth, and you found—what? Not that Mrs. What's-her-name—Horne—was a myth, as you expected, or conveniently—and, mind you, not unplausibly—dead, as I expected, but an actual, existent, highly respectable, though somewhat doting, old lady. She had you badly there, George my boy!"

"Yes," admitted George. "I wonder if she knew the woman was alive?"

"She chanced it; wished she might be dead, perhaps, but chanced it. That, George, is where Mrs. Witt is great."

"Mrs. Horne doesn't remember her being there in March, or indeed April."

"Perhaps not; but she doesn't say the contrary."

"Oh, no. She said that if the character says March, of course it was March."

"The 'of course' betrays a lay mind. But still the character does say March—for what it's worth."

"The copy of it does."

"I know what you mean. But think before you say that, George. It's pretty strong; and you haven't a tittle of evidence to support you."

"I don't want to say a word. I'll let them alone, if they'll let me alone. But that woman's Nelly Game, as sure as I'm——"

"An infernally obstinate chap," put in Mr. Blodwell.

Probably what George meant by being "let alone," was the cessation of paragraphs in the *Bull's-eye*. If so, his wish was not gratified. "Will Mr. George Neston"—George's name was no longer "withheld"—"retract?" took, in the columns of that publication, much the position occupied by *Delenda est Carthago* in the speeches of Cato the Elder. It met the reader on the middle page; it lurked for him in the leading article; it appeared, by way of playful reference, in the city intelligence; one man declared he found it in an advertisement, but this no doubt was an oversight—or perhaps a lie.

George was not more sensitive than other men, but the annoyance was extreme. The whole world seemed full of people reading the *Bull's-eye*, some with grave reprobation, some with offensive chucklings.

But if the *Bull's-eye* would not leave him alone, a large number of people did. He was not exactly cut; but his invitations diminished, the greetings he received grew less cordial than of yore: he was not turned out of the houses he went to, but he was not much pressed to come again. He was made to feel that right-minded and reasonable people—a term everybody uses to describe themselves—were against him, and that, if he wished to re-enter the good graces of society, he must do so by the strait and narrow gate of penitence and apology.

"I shall have to do it," he said to himself, as he sat moodily in his chambers. "They're all at me—uncle Roger, Tommy Myles, Isabel—all of them. I'm shot if I ever interfere with anybody's marriage again."

The defection of Isabel rankled in his mind worst of all. That she, of all people, should turn against him, and, as a last insult, send him upbraiding messages through Tommy Myles! This she had done, and George was full of wrath.

"A note for you, sir," said Timms, entering in his usual silent manner. Timms had no views on the controversy, being one of those rare people who mind their own business; and George had fallen so low as to be almost grateful for the colourless impartiality with which he bore himself towards the quarrel between his masters.

George took the note. "Mr. Gerald been here, Timms?"

"He looked in for letters, sir; but went away directly on hearing you were here."

Timms stated this fact as if it were in the ordinary way of friendly intercourse, and withdrew.

"Well, I am——!" exclaimed George, and paused.

The note was addressed in the handwriting he now knew very well, the handwriting of the Bournemouth character.

"DEAR MR. NESTON,

"I shall be alone at five o'clock to-day. Will you come and see me?

"Yours sincerely,
"NEAERA WITT."

"You must do as a lady asks you," said George, "even if she does steal shoes, and you have mentioned it. Here goes! What's she up to now, I wonder?"

Neaera, arrayed in the elaborate carelessness of a tea-gown, received him, not in the drawing-room, but in her own snuggery. Tea was on the table; there was a bright little fire, and a somnolent old cat snoozed on the hearth-rug. The whole air was redolent of what advertisements called a "refined home," and Neaera's manner indicated an almost pathetic desire to be friendly, checked only by the self-respecting fear of a rude rebuff to her advances.

"It is really kind of you to come," she said, "to consent to a parley."

"The beaten side always consents to a parley," answered George, taking the seat she indicated. She was half sitting, half lying on a sofa when he came in, and resumed her position after greeting him.

"No, no," she said quickly; "that's where it's hard—when you're beaten. But do you consider yourself beaten?"

"Up to now, certainly."

"And you really are not convinced?" she asked, eyeing him with a look of candid appeal to his better nature.

"It is your fault, Mrs. Witt."

"My fault?"

"Yes. Why are you so hard to forget?" George thought there was no harm in putting it in a pleasant way.

"Ah, why was Miss—now is it Game or Games?—so hard to forget?"

"It is, or rather was, Game. And I suppose she was hard to forget for the same reason as you—would be."

"And what is that?"

"If you ask my cousin, no doubt he will tell you."

Neaera smiled.

"What more can I do?" she asked. "Your people didn't know me. I have produced a letter showing I was somewhere else."

"Excuse me——"

"Well, well, then, a copy of a letter."

"What purports to be a copy."

"How glad I am I'm not a lawyer! It seems to make people so suspicious."

"It's a great pity you didn't keep the original."

Neaera said nothing. Perhaps she did not agree.

"But I suppose you didn't send for me to argue about the matter?"

"No. I sent for you to propose peace. Mr. Neston, I am so weary of fighting. Why will you make me fight?"

"It's not for my pleasure," said George.

"For whose, then?" she asked, stretching out her arms with a gesture of entreaty. "Cannot we say no more about it?"

"With all my heart."

"And you will admit you were wrong?"

"That is saying more about it."

"You cannot enjoy the position you are in."

"I confess that."

"Mr. Neston, do you never think it's possible you are wrong? But no, never mind. Will you agree just to drop it?"

"Heartily. But there's the *Bull's-eye*."

"Oh, bother the *Bull's-eye*! I'll go and see the editor," said Neaera.

"He's a stern man, Mrs. Witt."

"He won't be so hard to deal with as you. There, that's settled. Hurrah! Will you shake hands, Mr. Neston?"

"By all means."

"With a thief?"

"With you, thief or no thief. And I must tell you you are very——"

"What?"

"Well, above small resentments."

"Oh, what does it matter? Suppose I did take the boots?"

"Shoes," said George.

Neaera burst into a laugh. "You are very accurate."

"And you are very inaccurate, Mrs. Witt."

"I shall always be amused when I meet you. I shall know you have your hand on your watch."

"Oh yes. I retract nothing."

"Then it is peace?"

"Yes."

Neaera sat up and gave him her hand, and the peace was ratified. But it so chanced that Neaera's sudden movement roused the cat. He yawned and got up, arching his back, and digging his claws into the hearth-rug.

"Bob," said Neaera, "don't spoil the rug."

George's attention was directed to the animal, and, as he looked at it, he started. Bob's change of posture had revealed a serious deficiency: he had no tail, or the merest apology for a tail.

It was certainly an odd coincidence, perhaps nothing more, but a very odd coincidence, that George should have seen in the courtyard at Peckton Gaol no less than three tailless cats! Of course there are a good many in the world; but still most cats have tails.

"I like a black cat, don't you?" said Neaera. "He's nice and Satanic."

The Peckton cats were black, too,—black as ink or the heart of a money-lender.

"An old favourite?" asked George, insidiously.

"I've had him a good many years. Oh!"

The last word slipped from Neaera involuntarily.

"Why 'oh!'?"

"I'd forgotten his milk," answered Neaera, with extraordinary promptitude.

"Where did you get him?"

Neaera was quite calm again. "Some friends gave him me. Please don't say I stole my cat, too, Mr. Neston."

George smiled; indeed, he almost laughed. "Well, it is peace, Mrs. Witt," he said, taking his hat. "But remember!"

"What?" said Neaera, who was still smiling and cordial, but rather less at her ease than before.

"A cat may tell a tale, though he bear none."

"What do you mean?"

"If it is ever war again, I will tell you. Good-bye, Mrs. Witt."

"Good-bye. Please don't have poor Bob arrested. He didn't steal the boots—oh, the shoes, at any rate."

"I expect he was in prison already."

Neaera shook her head with an air of bewilderment. "I really don't understand you. But I'm glad we're not enemies any longer."

George departed, but Neaera sat down on the rug and gazed into the fire. Presently Bob came to look after the forgotten milk. He rubbed himself right along Neaera's elbow, beginning from his nose, down to the end of what he called his tail.

"Ah, Bob," said Neaera, "what do you want? Milk, dear? 'Good for evil, milk for——'"

Bob purred and capered. Neaera gave him his milk, and stood looking at him.

"How would you like to be drowned, dear?" she asked.

The unconscious Bob lapped on.

Neaera stamped her foot. "He shan't! He shan't! He shan't!" she exclaimed. "Not an inch! Not an inch!"

Bob finished his milk and looked up.

"No, dear, you shan't be drowned. Don't be afraid."

As Bob knew nothing about drowning, and only meant that he wanted more milk, he showed no gratitude for his reprieve. Indeed, seeing there was to be no more milk, he pointedly turned his back, and began to wash his face.

CHAPTER VIII.
THE FRACAS AT MRS. POCKLINGTON'S.

"I NEVER heard anything so absurd in all my life," said Mr. Blodwell, with emphasis.

George had just informed him of the treaty between himself and Neaera. He had told his tale with some embarrassment. It is so difficult to make people who were not present understand how an interview came to take the course it did.

"She seemed to think it all right," George said weakly.

"Do you suppose you can shut people's mouths in that way?"

"There are other ways," remarked George, grimly, for his temper began to go.

"There are," assented Mr. Blodwell; "and in these days, if you use them, it's five pounds or a month, and a vast increase of gossip into the bargain. What does Gerald say?"

"Gerald? Oh, I don't know. I suppose Mrs. Witt can manage him."

"Do you? I doubt it. Gerald isn't over easy to manage. Think of the position you leave him in!"

"He believes in her."

"Yes, but he won't be content unless other people do. Of course they'll say she squared you."

"Squared me!" exclaimed George, indignantly.

"Upon my soul, I'm not sure she hasn't."

"Of course you can say what you please, sir. From you I can't resent it."

"Come, don't be huffy. Bright eyes have their effect on everybody. By the way, have you seen Isabel Bourne lately?"

"No."

"Heard from her?"

"She sent me a message through Tommy Myles."

"Is he in her confidence?"

"Apparently. The effect of it was, that she didn't want to see me till I had come to my senses."

"In those words?"

"Those were Tommy's words."

"Then relations are strained?"

"Miss Bourne is the best judge of whom she wishes to see."

"Quite so," said Mr. Blodwell, cheerfully. "At present she seems to wish to see Myles. Well, well, George, you'll have to come to your knees at last."

"Mrs. Witt doesn't require it."

"Gerald will."

"Gerald be—— But I've never told you of my fresh evidence."

"Oh, you're mad! What's in the wind now?"

Five minutes later, George flung himself angrily out of Mr. Blodwell's chambers, leaving that gentleman purple and palpitating with laughter, as he gently re-echoed,

"The cat! Go to the jury on the cat, George, my boy!"

To George, in his hour of adversity, Mrs. Pocklington was as a tower of strength. She said that the Nestons might squabble among themselves as much as they liked; it was no business of hers. As for the affair getting into the papers, her visiting-list would suffer considerably if she cut out everybody who was wrongly or, she added significantly, rightly abused in the papers. George Neston might be mistaken, but he was an honest young man, and for her part she thought him an agreeable one—anyhow, a great deal too good for that insipid child, Isabel Bourne. If anybody didn't like meeting him at her house, they could stay away. Poor Laura Pocklington protested that she hated and despised George, but yet couldn't stay away.

"Then, my dear," said Mrs. Pocklington, tartly, "you can stay in the nursery."

"It's too bad!" exclaimed Laura. "A man who says such things isn't fit——"

Mrs. Pocklington shook her head gently. Mr. Pocklington's Radical principles extended no more to his household than to his business.

"Laura dear," she said, in pained tones, "I do so dislike argument."

So George went to dinner at Mrs. Pocklington's, and that lady, remorseless in parental discipline, sent Laura down to dinner with him; and, as everybody knows, there is nothing more pleasing and interesting than a pretty girl in a dignified pet. George enjoyed himself. It was a long time since he had flirted; but really now, considering Isabel's conduct, he felt at perfect liberty to conduct himself as seemed to him good. Laura was an old friend, and George determined to see how implacable her wrath was.

"It's so kind of you to give me this pleasure," he began.

"Pleasure?" said Laura, in her loftiest tone.

"Yes; taking you down, you know."

"Mamma made me."

"Ah, now you're trying to take me down."

"I wonder you can look any one in the face——"

"I always enjoy looking you in the face."

"After the things you've said about poor Neaera!"

"Neaera?"

"Why shouldn't I call her Neaera?"

"Oh, no reason at all. It may even be her name."

"A woman who backbites is bad, but a man——"

"Is the deuce?" said George inquiringly.

Laura tried another tack. "All your friends think you wrong, even mamma."

"What does that matter, as long as you think I'm right?"

"I don't; I don't. I think——"

"That it's great fun to torment a poor man who——"

George paused.

"Who what?" said Laura, with deplorable weakness.

"Values your good opinion very highly."

"Nonsense!"

George permitted himself to sigh deeply. A faint twitching betrayed itself about the corners of Laura's pretty mouth.

"If you want to smile, I will look away," said George.

"You're very foolish," said Laura; and George knew that this expression on a lady's lips is not always one of disapproval.

"I am, indeed," said he, "to spend my time in a vain pursuit."

"Of Neaera?"

"No, not of Neaera."

"I should never," said Laura, demurely, "have referred to Miss Bourne, if you hadn't, but as you have——"

"I didn't."

Presumably George explained whom he did refer to, and apparently the explanation took the rest of dinner-time. And as the ladies went upstairs, Mrs. Pocklington patted Laura's shoulder with an approving fan.

"There's a good child! It shows breeding to be agreeable to people you dislike."

Laura blushed a little, but answered dutifully, "I am glad you are pleased, mamma." Most likely she did not impose on Mrs. Pocklington. She certainly did not on herself.

George found himself left next to Sidmouth Vane.

"Hallo, Neston!" said that young gentleman, with his usual freedom. "Locked her up yet?"

George said Mrs. Witt was still at large. Vane had been his fag, and George felt he was entitled to take it out of him in after life whenever he could.

"Wish you would," continued Mr. Vane. "That ass of a cousin of yours would jilt her, and I would wait outside Holloway or Clerkenwell, or wherever they put 'em, and receive her sympathetically—hot breakfast, brass band, first cigar for six months, and all that, don't you know, like one of those Irish fellows."

"You have no small prejudices."

"Not much. A girl like that, *plus* an income like that, might steal all Northampton for what I care. Going upstairs?"

"Yes; there's an 'At Home' on, isn't there?"

"Yes, so I'm told. I shouldn't go, if I were you."

"Why the devil not?"

"Gerald's going to be there—told me so."

"Really, Vane, you're very kind. We shan't fight."

"I don't know about that. He's simply mad."

"Anything new?"

"Yes; he told me you'd been trying to square Mrs. Witt behind his back, and he meant to have it out with you."

"Well," said George, "I won't run. Come along."

The guests were already pouring in, and among the first George encountered was Mr. Dennis Espion, as over-strained as ever. Espion knew that George was aware of his position on the *Bull's-eye*.

"Ah, how are you, Neston?" he said, holding out his hand.

George looked at it for a moment, and then took it.

"I support life and your kind attentions, Espion."

"Ah! well, you know, we can't help it—a matter of public interest. I hope you see our position——"

"Yes," said George, urbanely; "*Il faut vivre.*"

"I don't suppose you value our opinion, but——"

"Oh yes; I value it at a penny—every evening."

"I was going to say——"

"Keep it, my dear fellow. What you say has market value—to the extent I have mentioned."

"My dear Neston, may I——"

"Consider this an interview? My dear Espion, certainly. Make any use of this communication you please. Good night."

George strolled away. "Suppose I was rather rude," he said to himself. "But, hang it, I must have earned that fellow fifty pounds!"

George was to earn Mr. Espion a little more yet, as it turned out. He had not gone many steps before he saw his cousin Gerald making his bow to Mrs. Pocklington. Mr. Espion saw him too, and was on the alert. Gerald was closely followed by Tommy Myles.

"Ah, the enemy!" exclaimed George under his breath, pursuing his way towards Laura Pocklington.

The throng was thick, and his progress slow. He had time to observe Gerald, who was now talking to Tommy and to Sidmouth Vane, who had joined them. Gerald was speaking low, but his gestures betrayed strong excitement. Suddenly he began to walk rapidly towards George, the people seeming to fall aside from his path. Tommy Myles followed him, while Vane all but ran to George and whispered eagerly,

"For God's sake, clear out, my dear fellow! He's mad! There'll be a shindy, as sure as you're born!"

George did not like shindies, especially in drawing-rooms; but he liked running away less. "Oh, let's wait and see," he replied.

Gerald was looking dangerous. The healthy ruddiness of his cheek had darkened to a deep flush, his eyes looked vicious, and his mouth was set. As he walked quickly up to his cousin, everybody tried to look away; but out of the corners of two hundred eyes eager glances centred on the pair.

"May I have a word with you?" Gerald began, calmly enough.

"As many as you like; but I don't know that this place——"

"It will do for what I have to say," Gerald interrupted.

"All right. What is it?"

"I want two things of you. First, you will promise never to dare to address my—Mrs. Witt again."

"And the second?" asked George.

"You will write and say you've told lies, and are sorry for it."

"I address whom I please and write what I please."

Vane interposed.

"Really, Neston—you, Gerald, I mean—don't make a row here. Can't you get him away, Tommy?"

Gerald gave Tommy a warning look, and poor Tommy shook his head mournfully.

George felt the necessity of avoiding a scene. He began to move quietly away. Gerald stood full in his path.

"You don't go till you've answered. Will you do what I tell you?"

"Really, Gerald," George began, still clinging to peace.

"Yes or no?"

"No," said George, with a smile and a shrug.

"Then, you cur, take——"

In another moment he would have struck George full in the face, but the vigilant Vane caught his arm as he raised it.

"You damned fool! Are you drunk?" he hissed into his ear. "Everybody's looking."

- 51 -

It was true. Everybody was.

"All the better," Gerald blurted out. "I'll thrash him——"

Tommy Myles ranged up and passed his hand through the angry man's other arm.

"Can't you go, George?" asked Vane.

"No," said George, calmly; "not till he's quiet."

The hush that had fallen on the room attracted Mrs. Pocklington's attention. In a moment, as it seemed, though her movements were as a rule slow and stately, she was beside them, just in time to see Gerald make a violent effort to throw off Vane's detaining hand.

"I cannot get anybody to go into the music-room," she said; "and the signora is waiting to begin. Mr. Neston, give me your arm, and we will show the way." Then her eyes seemed to fall for the first time on George. "Oh, you here too, Mr. George? Laura is looking for you everywhere. Do find her. Come, Mr. Neston. Mr. Vane, go and give your arm to a lady."

The group scattered, obedient to her commands, and everybody breathed a little sigh, half of relief, half of disappointment, and told one another that Mrs. Pocklington was a great woman.

"In another second," said Tommy Myles, as he restored himself with a glass of champagne, "it would have been a case of Bow Street!"

"I think it fairly amounts to a *fracas*," said Mr. Espion to himself; and as a *fracas*, accordingly, it figured.

CHAPTER IX.
GERALD NESTON SATISFIES HIMSELF.

ON the following morning, Lord Tottlebury sat as arbitrator, gave an impartial consideration to both sides of the question, and awarded that George should apologise for his charges, and Gerald for his violence. Lord Tottlebury argued the case with ability, and his final judgment was able and conclusive. Unfortunately, however, misled by the habit before mentioned of writing to the papers about matters other than those which immediately concerned him, Lord Tottlebury forgot that neither party had asked him to adjudicate, and, although Maud Neston was quite convinced by his reasoning, his award remained an opinion *in vacuo*; and the two clear and full letters which he wrote expressing his views were consigned by their respective recipients to the waste-paper basket. Each of the young men thanked Lord Tottlebury for his kind efforts, but feared that the unreasonable temper displayed by the other would render any attempt at an arrangement futile. Lord Tottlebury sighed, and sadly returned to his article on "What the Kaiser should do next." He was in a hurry to finish it, because he also had on hand a reply to Professor Dressingham's paper on "The Gospel Narrative and the Evolution of *Crustacea* in the Southern Seas."

After his outburst, Gerald Neston had allowed himself to be taken home quietly, and the next morning he had so far recovered his senses as to promise Sidmouth Vane that he would not again have recourse to personal violence. He said he had acted on a momentary impulse—which Vane did not believe,—and, at any rate, nothing of the kind need be apprehended again; but as for apologising, he should as soon think of blacking George's boots. In fact, he was, on the whole, well pleased with himself, and, in the course of the day, went off to Neaera to receive her thanks and approval.

He found her in very low spirits. She had been disappointed at the failure of her arrangement with George, and half inclined to rebel at Gerald's peremptory *veto* on any attempt at hushing up the question. She had timidly tried the line of pooh-poohing the whole matter, and Gerald had clearly shown her that, in his opinion, it admitted of no such treatment. She had not dared to ask him seriously if he would marry her, supposing the accusation were true. A joking question of the kind had been put aside as almost in bad taste, and, at any rate, ill-timed. Consequently she was uneasy, and ready to be very miserable on the slightest provocation. But to-day Gerald came in a different mood. He was triumphant, aggressive, and fearless; and before he had been in the room ten minutes, he broached his new design—a design that was to show conclusively the esteem in which he held the vile slanders and their utterer.

"Be married directly! Oh, Gerald!"

"Why not, darling? It will be the best answer to them."

"What would your father say?"

"I know he will approve. Why shouldn't he?"

"But—but everybody is talking about me."

"What do I care?"

It suits some men to be in love, and Gerald looked very well as he threw out his defiance *urbi et orbi*. Neaera was charmed and touched.

"Gerald dear, you are too good—you are, indeed,—too good to me and too good for me."

Gerald said, in language too eloquent to be reproduced, that nobody could help being "good" to her, and nobody in the world was good enough for her.

"And are you content to take me entirely on trust?"

"Absolutely."

"While I am under this shadow?"

"You are under no shadow. I take your word implicitly, as I would take it against gods and men."

"Ah, I don't deserve it."

"Who could look in your eyes"—Gerald was doing so—"and think of deceit? Why do you look away, sweetheart?"

"I daren't—I daren't!"

"What?"

"Be—be—trusted like that!"

Gerald smiled. "Very well; then you shan't be. I will treat you as if—as if I *doubted* you. Then will you be satisfied?"

Neaera tried to smile at this pleasantry. She was kneeling by Gerald's chair as she often did, looking up at him.

"Doubted me?" she said.

"Yes, since you won't let your eyes speak for you, I will put you to the question. Will that be enough?"

Poor Neaera! she thought it would be quite enough.

"And I will ask you, what I have never condescended to ask yet, dearest, if there's a word of truth in it all?" Gerald, still playfully, took one of her hands and raised it aloft. "Now look at me and say—what shall be your oath?"

Neaera was silent. This passed words; every time she spoke she made it worse.

"I know," pursued Gerald, who was much pleased with his little comedy. "Say this, 'On my honour and love, I am not the girl.'"

Why hadn't she let him alone with his nonsense about her eyes? That was not, to Neaera's thinking, as bad as a lie direct. "On her honour and love!" She could not help hesitating for just a moment.

"I am not the girl, on my honour and love." Her words came almost with a sob, a stifled sob, that made Gerald full of remorse and penitence, and loud in imprecations on his own stupidity.

"It was all a joke, sweetest," he pleaded; "but it was a stupid joke, and it has distressed you. Did you dream I doubted you?"

"No."

"Well, then, say you knew it was a joke."

"Yes, dear, I know it was,—of course it was; but it—it rather frightened me."

"Poor child! Never mind; you'll be amused when you think of it presently. And, my darling, it really, seriously, does make me happier. I never doubted, but it is pleasant to hear the truth from your own sweet lips. Now I am ready for all the world. And what about the day?"

"The day?"

"Of course you don't know what day! Shall it be directly?"

"What does 'directly' mean?" asked Neaera, mustering a rather watery smile.

"In a week."

"Gerald!"

But, after the usual negotiations, Neaera was brought to consent to that day three weeks, provided Lord Tottlebury's approval was obtained.

"And, please, don't quarrel with your cousin any more!"

"I can afford to let him alone now."

"And—— Are you going, Gerald?"

"No time to lose. I'm off to see the governor, and I shall come back and fetch you to dine in Portman Square. Good-bye for an hour, darling!"

"Gerald, suppose——"

"Well!"

"If—if—— No, nothing. Good-bye, dear; and——"

"What is it, sweet?"

"Nothing—well, and don't be long."

Gerald departed in raptures. As soon as he was out of the room, the tailless cat emerged from under the sofa. He hated violent motion of all kinds, and lovers are restless beings. Now, thank heaven! there was a chance of lying on the hearth-rug without being trodden upon!

"Did you hear that, Bob?" asked Neaera. "I—I went the whole hog, didn't I?"

Lord Tottlebury, who was much less inflexible than he seemed, did not hold out long against Gerald's vehemence, and the news soon spread that defiance was to be hurled in George's face. The *Bull's-eye* was triumphant. Isabel Bourne and Maud Neston made a hero of Gerald and a heroine of Neaera. Tommy Myles hastened to secure the position of "best man," and Sidmouth Vane discovered and acknowledged a deep worldly wisdom in Gerald's conduct.

"Of course," said he to Mr. Blodwell, on the terrace, "if it came out before the marriage, he'd stand pledged to throw her over, with the cash. But afterwards! Well, it won't affect the settlement, at all events."

Mr. Blodwell said he thought Gerald had not been actuated by this motive.

"Depend upon it, he has," persisted Vane. "Before marriage, the deuce! After marriage, a little weep and three months on the Riviera!"

"Oh, I suppose, if it came out after marriage, George would hold his tongue."

"Do you, by Jove? Then he'd be the most forgiving man in Europe. Why, he's been hunted down over the business—simply hunted down!"

"That's true. No, I suppose he'd be bound to have his revenge."

"Revenge! He'd have to justify himself."

Mr. Blodwell had the curiosity to pursue the subject with George himself.

"After the marriage? Oh, I don't know. I should like to score off the lot of them."

"Naturally," said Mr. Blodwell.

"At any rate, if I find out anything before, I shall let them have it. They haven't spared me."

"Anything new?"

"Yes. They've got the committee at the Themis to write and tell me that it's awkward to have Gerald and me in the same club."

"That's strong."

"I have to thank Master Tommy for that. Of course it means that I'm to go; but I won't. If they like to kick me out, they can."

"What's Tommy Myles so hot against you for?"

"Oh, those girls have got hold of him—Maud, and Isabel Bourne."

"Isabel Bourne?"

"Yes," said George, meeting Mr. Blodwell's questioning eye. "Tommy has a mind to try his luck there, I think."

"*Vice* you retired."

"Well, retired or turned out. It's like the army, you know; the two come to pretty much the same thing."

"You must console yourself, my boy," said Mr. Blodwell, slyly. He heard of most things, and he had heard of Mrs. Pocklington's last dinner-party.

"Oh, I'm an outcast now. No one would look at me."

"Don't be a humbug, George. Go and see Mrs. Pocklington, and, for heaven's sake let me get to my work."

It was Mr. Blodwell's practice to inveigle people into long gossips, and then abuse them for wasting his time; so George was not disquieted by the reproach. But he took the advice, and called in Grosvenor Square. He found Mrs. Pocklington in, but she was not alone. Her visitor was a very famous person, hitherto known to George only by repute,—the Marquis of Mapledurham.

The Marquis was well known on the turf and also as a patron of art, but it is necessary to add that more was known of him than was known to his advantage. In fact, he gave many people the opportunity of saying they would not count him among their acquaintances; and he gave very few of them the chance of breaking their word. He and Mrs. Pocklington amused one another, and, whatever he did, he never said anything that was open to complaint.

For some time George talked to Laura. Laura, having once come over to his side, was full of a convert's zeal, and poured abundant oil and wine into his wounds.

"How could I ever have looked at Isabel Bourne when she was there?" he began to think.

"Mr. Neston," said Mrs. Pocklington, "Lord Mapledurham wants to know whether you are *the* Mr. Neston."

"Mrs. Pocklington has betrayed me, Mr. Neston," said the Marquis.

"I am one of the two Mr. Nestons, I suppose," said George, smiling.

"Mr. George Neston?" asked the Marquis.

"Yes."

"And you let him come here, Mrs. Pocklington?"

"Ah, you know my house is a caravanserai. I heard you remark it yourself the other day."

"I shall go," said the Marquis, rising. "And, Mrs. Pocklington, I shall be content if you say nothing worse of my house. Good-bye, Miss Laura. Mr. Neston, I shall have a small party of bachelors to-morrow. It will be very kind if you will join us. Dinner at eight."

"See what it is to be an abused man," said Mrs. Pocklington, laughing.

"In these days the wicked must stand shoulder to shoulder," said the Marquis.

George accepted; in truth, he was rather flattered. And Mrs. Pocklington went away for quite a quarter of an hour. So that, altogether, he returned to the opinion that life is worth living, before he left the house.

CHAPTER X.
REMINISCENCES OF A NOBLEMAN.

ONCE upon a time, many years before this story begins, a certain lady said, and indeed swore with an oath, that Lord Mapledurham had promised to marry her, and claimed ten thousand pounds as damages for the breach of that promise. Lord Mapledurham said his memory was treacherous about such things, and he never contradicted a lady on a question of fact: but the amount which his society was worth seemed fairly open to difference of opinion, and he asked a jury of his countrymen to value it. This *cause célèbre*, for such it was in its day, did not improve Lord Mapledurham's reputation, but, on the other hand, it made Mr. Blodwell's. That gentleman reduced the damages to one thousand, and Lord Mapledurham said that his cross-examination of the plaintiff was quite worth the money. Since then, the two had been friends, and Mr. Blodwell prided himself greatly on his intimacy with such an exclusive person as the Marquis. George enjoyed his surprise at the announcement that they would meet that evening at the dinner-party.

"Why the dickens does he ask you?"

"Upon my honour, I don't know."

"It will destroy the last of your reputation."

"Oh, not if you are there, sir."

When George arrived at Lord Mapledurham's, he found nobody except his host and Mr. Blodwell.

"I must apologize for having nobody to meet you, Mr. Neston, except an old friend. I asked young Vane—whose insolence amuses me,—and Fitzderham, but they couldn't come."

"Three's a good number," said Mr. Blodwell.

"If they're three men. But two men and a woman, or two women and a man—awful!"

"Well, we are men, though George is a young one."

"I don't feel very young," said George, smiling, as they sat down.

"I am fifty-five," said the Marquis, "and I feel younger every day,—not in body, you know, for I'm chockful of ailments; but in mind. I am growing out of all the responsibilities of this world."

"And of the next?" asked Blodwell.

"In the next everything is arranged for us, pleasantly or otherwise. As to this one, no one expects anything more of me—no work, no good deeds, no career, no nothing. It's a delicious freedom."

"You never felt your bonds much."

"No; but they were there, and every now and then they dragged on my feet."

"Your view of old age is comforting," said George.

"Only, George, if you want to realize it, you must not marry," said Mr. Blodwell.

"No, no," said the Marquis. "By the way, Blodwell, why did you never marry?"

"Too poor, till too late," said Mr. Blodwell, briefly.

The Marquis raised his glass, and seemed to drink a respectful toast to a dead romance.

"And you, Lord Mapledurham?" George ventured to ask.

"Ay, ask him!" said Mr. Blodwell. "Perhaps his reason will be less sadly commonplace."

"I don't know," said the Marquis, pondering. "Some of them expected it, and that disgusted me. And some of them didn't, and that disgusted me too."

"You put the other sex into rather a difficult position," remarked George, laughing.

"Nothing to what they've put me into. Eh, Blodwell?"

"Now, tell me, Mapledurham," said Mr. Blodwell, who was in a serious mood to-night. "On the whole, have you enjoyed your life?"

"I have wasted opportunities, talents, substance—everything: and enjoyed it confoundedly. I am no use even as a warning."

"Ask a parson," said Mr. Blodwell, dryly.

"I remember," the Marquis went on, dreamily, "an old ruffian—another old ruffian—saying just the same sort of thing one night. I was at Liverpool for the Cup. Well, in the evening, I got tired of the other fellows, and went out for a turn; and down a back street, I found an old chap sitting on a doorstep,—a dirty old fellow, but uncommonly picturesque, with a long grey beard. As I came by, he was just trying to get up, but he staggered and fell back again."

"Drunk?" asked Mr. Blodwell.

The Marquis nodded. "I gave him a hand, and asked if I could do anything for him. 'Yes, give me a drink,' says he. I told him he was drunk already, but he said that made no odds, so I helped him to the nearest gin-palace."

"Behold this cynic's unacknowledged kindnesses!" said Mr. Blodwell.

"Sat him down in a chair, and gave him liquor.

"'Do you enjoy getting drunk?' I asked him, just as you asked me if I had enjoyed life.

"His drink didn't interfere with his tongue, it only seemed to take him in the legs. He put down his glass, and made me a little speech.

"'Liquor,' says he, 'has been my curse; it's broken up my home, spoilt my work, destroyed my character, sent me and mine to gaol and shame. God bless liquor! say I.'

"I told him he was an old beast, much as you, Blodwell, told me I was, in a politer way. He only grinned, and said, 'If you're a gentleman, you'll see me home. Lying in the gutter costs five shillings, next morning, and I haven't got it.'

"'All right,' said I; and after another glass we started out. He knew the way, and led me through a lot of filthy places to one of the meanest dens I ever saw. A red-faced, red-armed, red-voiced (you know what I mean) woman opened the door, and let fly a cloud of Billingsgate at him. The old chap treated her with lofty courtesy.

"'Quite true, Mrs. Bort,' says he; 'you're always right: I have ruined myself.'

"'And yer darter!' shrieked the woman.

"'And my daughter. And I am drunk now, and hope to be drunk to-morrow.'

"'Ah! you old beast!' said she, just as I had, shaking her fist.

"He turned round to me, and said, 'I am obliged to you, sir. I don't know your name.'

"'You wouldn't be better off if you did,' says I. 'You couldn't drink it.'

"'Will you give me a sovereign?' he asked. 'A week's joy, sir,—a week's joy and life.'

"'Give it me,' said the woman, 'then me and she'll get something to eat, to keep us alive.'

"I'm a benevolent man at bottom, Mr. Neston, as Blodwell remarks. I said,

"'Here's a sovereign for you and her' (I supposed she meant the daughter) 'to help in keeping you alive; and here's a sovereign for you, sir, to help in killing you—and the sooner the better, say I.'

"'You're right,' said he. 'The liquor's beginning to lose its taste. And when that's gone, Luke Gale's gone!'"

"Luke who?" burst from the two men.

Lord Mapledurham looked up. "What's the matter? Gale, I think. I found out afterwards that the old animal had painted water-colours—the only thing he had to do with water."

"The Lord hath delivered her into your hand," said Mr. Blodwell to George.

"Are you drunk too, Blodwell?" asked the Marquis.

"No; but——"

"What was the woman's name?" asked George, taking out a note-book.

"Bort. Going to tell me?"

"Well, if you don't mind——"

"Not a bit. Tell me later on, if it's amusing. There are so precious few amusing things."

"You didn't see the daughter, did you?"

"Oh, of course it's the daughter! No."

"Did you ever know a man named Witt?"

"Never; but, Mr. Neston, I have heard of a Mrs. Witt. Now, Blodwell, either out with it, or shut up and let's talk of something else."

"The latter, please," said Mr. Blodwell, urbanely.

And the Marquis, who had out-grown the vanity of desiring to know everything, made no effort to recur to the subject. Only, as George took his leave, he received a piece of advice, together with a cordial invitation to come again.

"Excuse me, Mr. Neston," said the Marquis. "I fancy I have given you some involuntary assistance to-night."

"I hope so. I shall know in a day or two."

"To like to be right, Mr. Neston, is the last weakness of a wise man; to like to be thought right is the inveterate prejudice of fools."

"That last is a hard saying, my lord," said George, with a laugh.

"It really depends mostly on your income," answered the Marquis. "Good-night, Mr. Neston."

George said good-night, and walked off, shrugging his shoulders at the thought that even so acute a man as Lord Mapledurham seemed unable to appreciate his position.

"They all want me to drop it," he mused. "Well, I will, unless——! But to-morrow I'll go to Liverpool."

He was restless and excited. Home and bed seemed unacceptable, and he turned into the Themis Club, whence the machinations of the enemy had not yet ejected him. There, extended on a sofa and smoking a cigar, he found Sidmouth Vane.

"Why didn't you come to Lord Mapledurham's, Vane?" asked George.

"Oh, have you been there? I was dining with my chief. I didn't know you knew Mapledurham."

"I met him yesterday for the first time."

"He's a queer old sinner," said Vane. "But have you heard the news?"

"No. Is there any?"

"Tommy Myles has got engaged."

George started. He had a presentiment of the name of the lady.

"Pull yourself together, my dear boy," continued Vane. "Bear it like a man."

"Don't be an ass, Vane. I suppose it's Miss Bourne?"

Vane nodded. "It would really be amusing," he said, "if you'd tell me honestly how you feel. But, of course, you won't. You've begun already to look as if you'd never heard of Miss Bourne."

"Bosh!" said George.

"Now, I always wonder why fellows do that. When I've been refused by a girl, and——"

"I beg your pardon," said George. "I haven't been refused by Miss Bourne."

"Well, you would have been, you know. It comes to the same thing."

George laughed. "I dare say I should; but I never meant to expose myself to such a fate."

"George, my friend, do you think you're speaking the truth?"

"I am speaking the truth."

"Not a bit of it," responded Vane, calmly. "A couple of months ago you meant to ask her; and, what's more, she'd have had you."

George was dimly conscious that this might be so.

"It isn't my moral," Vane went on.

"Your moral?"

"No. I took it from the *Bull's-eye.*"

George groaned.

"They announce the marriage to-night, and add that they have reason to believe that the engagement has come about largely through the joint interest of the parties in *l'affaire Neston.*"

"I should say they are unusually accurate."

"Meaning thereby, to those who have eyes, that she's jilted you because of your goings-on, and taken up with Tommy. In consequence, you are to-night 'pointing a moral and adorning a tale.'"

"The devil!"

"Yes, not very soothing, is it? But so it is. I looked in at Mrs. Pocklington's, and they were all talking about it."

"The Pocklingtons were?"

"Yes. And they asked me——"

"Who asked you?"

"Oh, Violet Fitzderham and Laura Pocklington,—if it was the fact that you were in love with Miss Bourne."

"And what did you say?"

"I said it was matter of notoriety."

"Confound your gossip! There's not a word of truth in it."

"I didn't say there was. I said it was a matter of notoriety. So it was."

"And did they believe it?"

"Did who believe it?" asked Vane, smiling slightly.

"Oh, Miss Pocklington, and—and the other girl."

"Yes, Miss Pocklington and the other girl, I think, believed it."

"What did they say?"

"The other girl said it served you right."

"And——?"

"And Miss Pocklington said it was time for some music."

"Upon my soul, it's too bad!"

"My dear fellow, you know you were in love with her—in your fishlike kind of way. Only you've forgotten it. One does forget it when——"

"Well?" asked George.

"When one's in love with another girl. Ah, George, you can't escape my eagle eye! I saw your game, and I did you a kindness."

George thought it no use trying to keep his secret. "That's your idea of a kindness, is it?"

"Certainly. I've made her jealous."

"Really," said George, haughtily, "I think this discussion of ladies' feelings is hardly in good taste."

"Quite right, old man," answered Vane, imperturbably. "It's lucky that didn't strike you before you'd heard all you wanted to."

"I say, Vane," said George, leaning forward, "did she seem——"

"Miss Pocklington, or the other girl?"

"Oh, damn the other girl! Did she, Vane, old boy?"

"Yes, she did, a little, George, old boy."

"I'm a fool," said George.

"Oh, I don't know," said Vane, tolerantly. "I'm always a fool myself about these things."

"I must go and see them to-morrow. No, I can't go to-morrow; I have to go out of town."

"Ah! where?"

"Liverpool, on business."

"Liverpool, on business! Dear me! I'll tell you another odd thing, George,— a coincidence."

"Well?"

"You're going to Liverpool to-morrow on business. Well, to-day, Mrs. Witt went to Liverpool on business."

"The devil!" said George, for the second time.

CHAPTER XI.
PRESENTING AN HONEST WOMAN.

TO fit square pegs into round holes is one of the favourite pastimes of Nature. She does it roughly, violently, and with wanton disregard of the feelings of the square pegs. When, in her relentless sport, she has at last driven the poor peg in and made it fit, by dint of knocking off and abrading all its corners, philosophers glorify her, calling the process evolution, and plain men wonder why she did not begin at the other end, and make the holes square to fit the pegs.

The square peg on which these trite reflections hang is poor Neaera Witt. Nature made her a careless, ease-loving, optimistic creature, only to drive her, of malice prepense, into an environment—that is to say, in unscientific phrase, a hole—where she had need of the equipment of a full-blooded conspirator.

She resisted the operation; she persistently trusted to chance to extricate her from the toils into which she, not being a philosopher, thought chance had thrown her. If she saw a weapon ready to her hand, she used it, as she had used the Bournemouth character, but for the most part she trusted to luck. George Neston would fail, or he would relent; or Gerald would be invincibly incredulous, or, she would add, smiling at her face in the glass, invincibly in love. Somehow or other matters would straighten themselves out; and, at the worst, ten days more would bring the marriage; and after the marriage—— But really, ten days ahead is as far as one can be expected to look, especially when the ten days include one's wedding.

Nevertheless, Sidmouth Vane had a knack of being correct in his information, and he was correct in stating that Neaera had gone to Liverpool on business. It was, of course, merely a guess that her errand might be connected with George's, but it happened to be a right guess. Neaera knew well the weak spot in her armour. Hitherto she had been content to trust to her opponent not discovering it; but, as the decisive moment came nearer, a nervous restlessness so far overcame her natural *insouciance* as to determine her to an effort to complete her defences, in anticipation of any assault upon them. She was in happy ignorance of the chance that had directed George's forces against her vulnerable point, and imagined that she herself was, in all human probability, the only person in London to whom the name of Mrs. Bort would be more than an unmeaning uneuphonious syllable. To her the name was full of meaning; for, from her youth till the day of the happy intervention of that stout and elderly *deus ex machina*, the late Mr. Witt, Mrs. Bort had been to Neaera the impersonation of virtue and morality, and the physical characteristics that had caught Lord Mapledurham's frivolous attention had been to her merely the frowning aspect under which justice and righteousness are apt to present themselves.

Neaera was a good-hearted girl, and Mrs. Bort now lived on a comfortable pension, but no love mingled with the sense of duty that inspired the gift. Mrs. Bort had interpreted her quasi-maternal authority with the widest latitude, and Neaera shuddered to remember how often Mrs. Bort's discipline had made her smart, in a way, against which apathy of conscience was no shield or buckler. Recorder Dawkins would have groaned to know how even judicial terrors paled in Neaera's recollection before the image of Mrs. Bort.

These childish fears are hard to shake off, and Neaera, as she sped luxuriously to Liverpool, acknowledged to herself that, in that dreadful presence, no adventitious glories of present wealth or future rank would avail her. The governing fact in the situation, the fact that Neaera did not see her way to meet, was that Mrs. Bort was an honest woman. Neaera knew her, and knew that a bribe would be worse than useless, even if she dared to offer it.

"And I don't think," said Neaera, resting her pretty chin upon her pretty hand, "that I should dare." Then she laughed ruefully. "I'm not at all sure she wouldn't beat me; and if she did, what could I do?"

Probably Neaera exaggerated even the fearless rectitude of Mrs. Bort, but she was so convinced of the nature of the reception which any proposal of the obvious kind would meet with that she made up her mind that her only course was to throw herself on Mrs. Bort's mercy, in case that lady proved deaf to a subtle little proposal which was Neaera's first weapon.

So far as Neaera knew, Peckton and Manchester were the only places in which George Neston was likely to seek for traces of her. Liverpool, though remote from Peckton, was uncomfortably near Manchester. Every day now had great value. If she could get Mrs. Bort away to some remote spot as soon as might be, she gained no small advantage in her race against time and George Neston.

"If she will only go to Glentarroch, he will never find her."

Glentarroch was the name of a little retreat in remote Scotland, whither Mr. Witt had been wont to betake himself for rest and recreation. It was Neaera's now. It was a beautiful place, which was immaterial, and a particularly inaccessible one, which was most material. Would not Mrs. Bort's despotic instincts lead her to accept an invitation to rule over Glentarroch? Neaera could not afford to pity the hapless wights over whom Mrs. Bort would rule.

Mrs. Bort received Neaera in a way most unbecoming to a pensioner. "Well, Nery," she said, "what brings you here? No good, I'll be bound. Where's your mourning?"

Neaera said that she thought resignation to Heaven's will not a subject of reproach, and that she came to ask a favour of Mrs. Bort.

"Ay, you come to me when you want something. That's the old story."

Neaera remembered that Mrs. Bort had often taken her own view of what the supplicant wanted, and given something quite other than what was asked; but, in spite of this unpromising opening, she persevered, and laid before Mrs. Bort a dazzling picture of the grandeur waiting her at Glentarroch.

"And I shall be so much obliged. Really, I don't know what the servants— the girls, especially—may be doing."

"Carryings-on, I'll be bound," said Mrs. Bort. "Why don't you go yourself, Nery?"

"Oh, I can't, indeed. I—I must stay in London."

"Nasty, cold, dull little place it sounds," said Mrs. Bort.

"Oh, of course I shall consider all that——"

"He—he!" Mrs. Bort sniggered unpleasantly. "So it ain't sech a sweet spot, as ye call it, after all?"

Neaera recovered herself without dignity, and stated that she thought of forty pounds a year and all found.

"Ah, if I knowed what you was at, Nery!"

Neaera intimated that it was simply a matter of mutual accommodation. "And there's really no time to be lost," she said, plaintively. "I'm being robbed every day."

"Widows has hard times," said Mrs. Bort. And Neaera did not think it necessary to say how soon her hard times were coming to an end.

"Come agin to-morrer afternoon, and I'll tell ye," was Mrs. Bort's ultimatum. "And mind you don't get into mischief."

"Why afternoon?" asked Neaera.

"'Cause I'm washing," said Mrs. Bort, snappishly. "That's why."

Neaera in vain implored an immediate answer. Mrs. Bort said a day could not matter, and that, if Neaera pressed her farther, she should consider it an indication that something was "up," and refuse to go at all. Neaera was silenced, and sadly returned to her hotel.

"How I hate that good, good woman!" she cried. "I'll never see her again as long as I live, after to-morrow. Oh, I should like to hit her!"

The propulsions of cause upon cause are, as Bacon has said, infinite. If Mrs. Bort had not washed—in the technical sense, of course—on that particular Friday, Neaera would have come and gone—perhaps even Mrs. Bort might have gone too—before the train brought George Neston to Liverpool, and his eager inquiries landed him at Mrs. Bort's abode. As it was, Mrs. Bort's little servant bade him wait in the parlour, as her mistress was talking to a female in the kitchen. The little servant thought "female" the politest possible way of describing any person who was not a man, and accorded the title to Neaera on account of her rustling robes and gold-tipped parasol.

George did not question his informant, thereby showing that he, in the *rôle* of detective, was a square peg in a round hole. He heard proceeding from the kitchen a murmur of two subdued voices, one of which, however, dominated the other.

"That must be Mrs. Bort," thought he. "I wish I could hear the female."

Then his attention wandered, for he made sure the unknown could not be Neaera, as she had had a day's start of him. He did not allow for Mrs. Bort's washing. Suddenly the dominant voice was raised to the pitch of distinctness.

"Have ye told him," it said, "or have ye lied to him, as you lied to me yesterday?"

"I didn't—I didn't," was the answer. "You never asked me if I was going to be married."

"Oh, go along! You know how I'd have answered that when ye lived with me."

"How's that?" asked George, with a slight smile.

"Have ye told him?"

"Told him what?" asked Neaera; for it was clearly Neaera.

"Told him you're a thief."

"This woman's a brute," thought George.

"Have ye?"

"No, not exactly. How dare you question me?"

"Dare!" said Mrs. Bort; and George knew she was standing with her arms akimbo. "Dare!" she repeated *crescendo*; and apparently her aspect was threatening, for Neaera cried,

"Oh, I didn't mean that. Do let me go."

"Tell the truth, if your tongue'll do it. The truth, will ye?"

"The deuce!" said George; for, following on this last speech, he heard a sob.

"No, I haven't. I—oh, do have mercy on me!"

"Mercy! It's not mercy, it's a stick you want. But I'll tell him."

"Ah, stop, for Heaven's sake!"

There was a little scuffle; then the door flew open, and Mrs. Bort appeared, with Neaera clinging helplessly about her knees.

George rose and bowed politely. "I'm afraid I intrude," said he.

"That's easy mended," said Mrs. Bort, with significance.

Neaera had leapt up on seeing him, and leant breathless against the door, looking like some helpless creature at bay.

"Who let you in?" demanded the lady of the house.

"Your servant."

"I'll let *her* in," said Mrs. Bort, darkly. "Who are ye?"

George looked at Neaera. "My name is Neston," he said blandly.

"Neston?"

"Certainly."

"Then you're in nice time; I wanted you, young man. D'ye see that woman?"

"Certainly; I see Mrs. Witt."

"D'ye know what she is? Time you did, if you're a-going to take her to church."

Neaera started.

"I hope to do so," said George, smiling; "and I think I know all about her."

"Do ye, now? Happen ever to have heard of Peckton?"

Neaera buried her face in her hands, and cried.

"Ah, pity you haven't something to cry for! Thought I'd see a sin done for ten pound a month, did ye?"

George interposed; he began to enjoy himself. "Peckton? Oh yes. The shoes, you mean?"

Mrs. Bort gasped.

"A trifle," said George, waving the shoes into limbo.

"Gracious! You ain't in the same line, are you?"

George shook his head.

"Anything else?" he asked, still smiling sweetly.

"Only a trifle of forging," said Mrs. Bort. "But p'raps she got her deserts from me over that."

"Forging?" said George. "Oh ah, yes. You mean about——"

"Her place at Bournemouth? Ah, Nery, don't you ache yet?"

Apparently Neaera did. She shivered and moaned.

"But I've got it," continued Nemesis; and, she bounded across the room to a cupboard. "There, read that."

George took it calmly, but read it with secret eagerness. It was the original character, and stated that Miss Gale began her service in May, not March, 1883.

"I caught her a-copying it, and altering dates. My, how I did——"

"Dear, dear!" interrupted George. "I was afraid it was something new. Anything else, Mrs. Bort?"

Mrs. Bort was beaten.

"Go along," she said. "If you likes it, it's nothing to me. But lock up your money-box."

"Let me congratulate you, Mrs. Bort, on having done your duty."

"I'm an honest woman," said Mrs. Bort.

"Yes," answered George, "by the powers you are!" Then, turning to Mrs. Witt, he added, "Shall we go—Neaera dear?"

"You'll both of you die on the gallows," said Mrs. Bort.

"Come, Neaera," said George.

She took his arm and they went out, George giving the little servant a handsome tip to recompense her for the prospect of being "let in" by her mistress.

George's cab was at the door. He handed Neaera in. She was still half-crying and said nothing, except to tell him the name of her hotel. Then he raised his hat, and watched her driven away, wiping his brow with his handkerchief.

"Pheugh!" said he, "I've done it now—and what an infernal shame it is!"

CHAPTER XII.
NOT BEFORE THOSE GIRLS!

IT is a notorious fact that men of all ages and conditions quarrel, and quarrel sometimes with violence. Women also, of a low social grade, are not strangers to discord, and the pen of satire has not spared the tiffs and wrangles that arise between elderly ladies of irreproachable position, and between young ladies of possibly not irreproachable morals. It is harder to believe, harder especially for young men whose beards are yet soft upon their chins, that graceful gentle girlhood quarrels too. Nobody would believe it, if there were not sisters in the world; but, unhappily, in spite of the natural tendency to suppose that all attributes distinctively earthy are confined to his own sisters, and have no place in the sisters of his friends, a man of reflection, checking his observations in the various methods suggested by logicians, is forced to conclude that here is another instance of the old truth, that a thing is not to be considered non-existent merely because it is not visible to a person who is not meant to see it. This much apology for the incident which follows is felt to be necessary in the interest of the narrator's reputation for realism.

The fact is that there had been what reporters call a "scene" at Mrs. Pocklington's. It so fell out that Isabel Bourne, accompanied by Maud Neston, called on Laura to receive congratulations. Laura did her duty, felicitated her friend on Tommy in possession and Tommy's title in reversion, and loyally suppressed her personal opinion on the part these two factors had respectively played in producing the announced result. Her forbearance was ill-requited; for Maud, by way of clinching the matter and conclusively demonstrating the satisfactory position of affairs, must needs remark, "And what a lesson it will be for George!"

Laura said nothing.

"Oh, you mustn't say that, dear," objected Isabel. "It's really not right."

"I shall say it," said Maud; "it's so exactly what he deserves, and I know he feels it himself."

"Did he tell you so?" asked Laura, pausing in the act of pouring out tea.

Maud laughed.

"Hardly, dear. Besides, we are not on speaking terms. But Gerald and Mr. Myles both said so."

"Gerald and Mr. Myles!" said Laura.

"Please, don't talk about it," interposed Isabel. "What has happened made no difference."

"Why, Isabel, you couldn't have him after——"

"No," said Isabel; "but perhaps, Maud, I shouldn't have had him before."

"Of course you wouldn't, dear. You saw his true character."

"You never actually refused him, did you?" inquired Laura.

"No, not exactly."

"Then what did you say?"

"What did I say?"

"Yes, when he asked you, you know," said Laura, with a little smile.

Isabel looked at her suspiciously. "He never did actually ask me," she said, with dignity.

"Oh! I thought you implied——"

"But, of course, she knew he wanted to," Maud put in. "Didn't you, dear?"

"Well, I thought so," said Isabel, modestly.

"Yes, I know you thought so," said Laura. "Indeed, everybody saw that. Was it very hard to prevent him?"

Isabel's colour rose. "I don't know what you mean, Laura," she said.

Laura smiled with an unpleasantness that was quite a victory over nature. "Men sometimes fancy," she remarked, "that girls are rather in a hurry to think they want to propose."

"Laura!" exclaimed Maud.

"They even say that the wish is father to the thought," continued Laura, still smiling, but now a little tremulously.

Isabel grew more flushed. "I don't understand you. One would think you meant that I had run after him."

Laura remained silent.

"Everybody knows he was in love with Isabel for years," said Maud, indignantly.

"He was very patient," said Laura.

Isabel rose. "I shall not stay here to be insulted. It's quite obvious, Laura, why you say such things."

"I don't say anything. Only——"

"Well?"

"The next time, you might mention that among the reasons why you refused Mr. Neston was, that he never asked you."

"I see what it is," said Isabel. "Don't you, Maud?"

"Yes," said Maud.

"What is it?" demanded Laura.

"Oh, nothing. Only, I hope—I wish you joy of him."

"If you don't mind a slanderer," added Maud.

"It's not true!" said Laura. "How dare you say it?"

"Take care, dear, that he doesn't fancy you're in a hurry—— What was your phrase?" said Isabel.

"It's perfectly shameful," said Maud.

"I don't choose to hear a friend run down for nothing," declared Laura.

"A friend? How very chivalrous you are! Come, Maud dear."

"Good-bye, Laura," said Maud. "I'm sure you'll be sorry when you come to think."

"No, I shan't. I——"

"There!" said Isabel. "I do not care to be insulted any more."

The two visitors swept out, and Laura was left alone. Whereupon she began to cry. "I do hate that sort of vulgarity," said she, mopping her eyes. "I don't believe he ever thought——"

Mrs. Pocklington entered in urbane majesty. "Well, is Isabel pleased with her little man?" she asked. "Why, child, what's the matter?"

"Nothing," said Laura.

"You're crying."

"No, I'm not. Those girls have been horrid."

"What about?"

"Oh, the engagement, and——"

"And what?"

"And poor Mr. Neston—George Neston."

"Oh, poor George Neston. What did they say?"

"Isabel pretended he had been in love with her, and—and was in love with her, and that she had refused him."

"Oh, and that made you cry?"

"No—not that——"

"What, then?"

"Oh, please, mamma!"

Mrs. Pocklington smiled. "Stop crying, my dear. It used to suit me, but it doesn't suit you. Stop, dear."

"Very well, mamma," said poor Laura, thinking it a little hard that she might not even cry.

"Did you cry before the girls?"

"No," said Laura, with emphasis.

"Good child," said Mrs. Pocklington. "Now, listen to me. You're never to think of him again——"

"Mamma!"

"Till I tell you."

"Ah!"

"A tiresome, meddlesome fellow. Is your father in, Laura?"

"Yes, dear. Are you going to see him about——?"

"Why, you're as bad as Isabel!" said Mrs. Pocklington, with feigned severity, disengaging Laura's arms from her neck. "He's never asked you either!"

"No, dear; but——"

"The vanity of these children! There, let me go; and for goodness' sake, don't be a cry-baby, Laura. Men hate water-bottles."

Thus mingling consolation and reproof, Mrs. Pocklington took her way to her husband's study.

"I want five minutes, Robert," she said, sitting down.

"It's worth a thousand pounds a minute, my dear," said Mr. Pocklington, genially, laying down his pipe and his papers. "What with this strike——"

"Strike!" said Mrs. Pocklington with indignation. "Why do you let them strike, Robert?"

"I can't help it. They want more money."

"Nonsense! They want to be taught their Catechisms. But I didn't come to talk about that."

"I'm sorry you didn't, my dear. Your views are refreshing."

"Robert, Laura's got a fancy in her head about young George Neston."

"Oh!"

"'Oh!' doesn't tell me much."

"Well, you know all about him."

"He's a very excellent young man. Not rich."

"A pauper?"

"No. Enough."

"All right. If you're satisfied, I am. But hasn't he been making a fool of himself about some woman?"

"Really, Robert, how strangely you express yourself! I suppose you mean about Neaera Witt?"

"Yes, that's it. I heard some rumour."

"Heard some rumour! Of course you read every word about it, and gossiped over it at the Club and the House. Now, haven't you?"

"Perhaps I have," her husband admitted. "I think he's a young fool."

"Am I to consider it an obstacle?"

"Well, what do you think yourself?"

"It's your business. Men know about that sort of thing."

"Is the child—eh?"

"Yes, rather."

"And he?"

"Oh, yes, or will be very soon, when he sees she is."

"Poor little Lally!" said Mr. Pocklington. Then he sat and pondered. "It is an obstacle," he said at last.

"Ah!" said his wife.

"He must put himself right."

"Do you mean, prove what he says?"

"Well, at any rate, show he had good excuse for saying it."

"I think it's a little hard. But it's for you to decide."

Mr. Pocklington nodded.

"Then, that's settled," said Mrs. Pocklington. "It's a great comfort, Robert, to have a man who knows his mind on the premises."

"Be gentle with her," said he, and returned to the strike.

The other parties to the encounter over George's merits had by a natural impulse taken themselves to Neaera Witt's, with the hope of being thanked for their holy zeal. They were disappointed, for, on arriving at Albert Mansions, they were informed that Neaera, although returned from Liverpool, was not visible. "Mr. Neston has been waiting over an hour to see her, miss," said Neaera's highly respectable handmaid, "but she won't leave her room."

Gerald heard their voices, and came out.

"I can't think what's the matter," he said.

"Oh, I suppose the journey has knocked her up," suggested Isabel.

"Are you going to wait, Gerald?" asked Maud.

"Well, no. The fact is, she sent me a message to go away."

"Then come home with me," said Isabel, "and we will try to console you." Gerald would enjoy their tale quite as much as Neaera.

Low spirits are excusable in persons who are camping on an active volcano, and Neaera felt that this was very much her position. At any moment she might be blown into space, her pleasant dreams shattered, her champions put to shame, and herself driven for ever from the only place in life she cared to occupy. Her abasement was pitiful, and her penitence, being born merely of defeat, offers no basis of edification. She had serious thoughts of running away; for she did not think she could face Gerald's wrath, or, worse still, his grief. He would cast her off, and society would cast her off, and those dreadful papers would turn their thunders against her. She might have consoled herself for banishment from society with Gerald's love, or, perhaps, for loss of his love with the triumphs of society; but she would lose both, and have not a soul in the whole world to speak to except that hateful Mrs. Bort. So she sat and dolefully mused, with the tailless cat, that gift of a friendly gaoler at Peckton prison, purring on the rug before her, unconsciously personifying an irrevocable past and a future emptied of delight.

CHAPTER XIII.
CONTAINING MORE THAN ONE ULTIMATUM.

IT was fortunate that Mr. Blodwell was not very busy on Saturday morning, or he might have resented the choice of his chambers for a council, and not been mollified by being asked to take part in the deliberations. At eleven o'clock in the morning, Gerald Neston arrived, accompanied by Sidmouth Vane and Mr. Lionel Fitzderham, who was, in the first place, Mrs. Pocklington's brother, and, in the second place, chairman of the committee of the Themis Club.

"We have come, sir," said Gerald, "to ask you to use your influence with George. His conduct is past endurance."

"Anything new?" asked Mr. Blodwell.

"No, that's just it. This is Saturday. I'm to be married on Monday week; and George does nothing."

"What do you want him to do?"

"Why, to acknowledge himself wrong, as he can't prove himself right."

Mr. Blodwell looked at Fitzderham.

"Yes," said the latter. "It can't stay as it is. The lady must be cleared, if she can't be proved guilty. We arrived clearly at that conclusion."

"We?"

"The committee of the Themis."

"Oh, ah, yes. And you, Vane?"

"I concur," said Vane, briefly. "I've backed George up to now: but I agree he must do one thing or the other."

"Well, gentlemen, I suppose you're right. Only, if he won't?"

"Then we shall take action," said Fitzderham.

"So shall I," said Gerald.

Vane shrugged his shoulders.

Mr. Blodwell rang the bell.

"Is Mr. George in, Timms?" he asked.

"Yes, sir; just arrived."

"Ask him to step in to me, if he will. I don't see," he continued, "why you shouldn't settle it with him. I've nothing to do with it, thank God."

George entered. He was surprised to see the deputation, but addressed himself exclusively to Blodwell.

"Here I am, sir. What is it?"

"These gentlemen," said Mr. Blodwell, "think that the time has come for you to withdraw your allegations or to prove them."

"You see, George," said Vane, "it's not fair to leave Mrs. Witt under this indefinite stigma."

"Far from it," said Fitzderham.

George stood with his back against the mantel-piece. "I quite agree," he said. "Let's see—to-day's Saturday. When is the wedding, if there——?"

"Monday week," said Blodwell, hastily, fearing an explosion from Gerald.

"Very well. On Tuesday——"

"A telegram for you, sir," said Timms, entering.

"Excuse me," said George.

He opened and read his telegram. It ran, "Yes—my handwriting. Will return by next post registered—Horne, Bournemouth."

"On Monday," continued George, "at five o'clock in the afternoon, I will prove all I said, or withdraw it."

Gerald looked uneasy, but he tried to think, or at least to appear to think, that George's delay was only to make his surrender less abrupt.

"Very well! Shall we meet here?"

"No," said Gerald. "Mrs. Witt ought to be present."

"Is that desirable?" asked George.

"Of course it is."

"As you please. I should say not. But ask her, and be guided by her wishes."

"Well, then, at Lord Tottlebury's?" suggested Vane.

"By all means," said George. And, with a slight nod, he left the room.

"I hope," said Mr. Blodwell, "that you have done well in forcing matters to an extremity."

"Couldn't help it," said Vane, briefly.

And the council broke up.

Mrs. Horne's telegram made George's position complete. It was impossible for Neaera to struggle against such evidence, and his triumph was assured from the moment when he produced the original document and contrasted it with Neaera's doctored copy. Besides, Mrs. Bort was in the background, if necessary; and although an impulse of pity had led him to shield Neaera at Liverpool, he was in no way debarred by that from summoning Mrs. Bort to his assistance if he wanted her. The Neston honour was safe, an impostor exposed, and the cause of morality, respectability, truth, and decency powerfully forwarded. Above all, George himself was enabled to rout his enemies, to bring a blush to the unblushing cheek of the *Bull's-eye*, and to meet his friends without feeling that perhaps they were ashamed to be seen talking to him.

The delights of the last-mentioned prospect were so great, that George could not make up his mind to postpone them, and, in the afternoon, he set out to call on the Pocklingtons. There could be no harm in giving them at least a hint of the altered state of his fortunes, due, as it was in reality, to Mrs. Pocklington's kindness in presenting him to Lord Mapledurham. It would certainly be very pleasant to prove to the Pocklingtons, especially to Laura Pocklington, that they had been justified in standing by him, and that he was entitled, not to the good-natured tolerance accorded to honesty, but to the admiration due to success.

In matters of love, at least, George Neston cannot be presented as an ideal hero. Heroes unite the discordant attributes of violence and constancy: George had displayed neither. Isabel Bourne had satisfied his judgment without stirring his blood. When she presumed to be so ill-advised as to side against him, he resigned, without a pang, a prospect that had become almost a habit. Easily and insensibly the pretty image of Laura Pocklington had filled the vacant space. As he wended his way to Mrs. Pocklington's, he smiled to think that a month or two ago he had looked forward to a life spent with Isabel Bourne with acquiescence, though not, it is true, with rapture. Had the rapture existed before, it is sad to think that perhaps the smile would have been broader now; for love, when born in trepidation and nursed in joy, is often buried without lamentation and remembered with amusement—kindly, even tender amusement, but still amusement. An easy-going fancy like George's for Isabel cannot claim even the tribute of a tear behind the smile—a tear which, by its presence, causes yet another smile. George was not even grateful to Isabel for a pleasant dream and a gentle awakening. She was gone; and, what is more, she ought never to have come: and there was an end of it.

George, having buried Isabel, rang the bell with a composed mind. He might ask Laura Pocklington to marry him to-day, or he might not. He would be guided by circumstances in that matter: but at any rate he would ask her, and that soon; for she was the only girl he could ever be happy with, and, if he dawdled, his chance might be gone. Of course there was a crowd of suitors at her feet, and, although George had no unduly modest view of his own claims, he felt it behoved him to be up and doing. It is true that the crowd of suitors was not very much in evidence, but who could doubt its existence without questioning the sanity and eyesight of mankind?

As it so chanced, however, George did not see Laura. He saw Mrs. Pocklington, and that lady at once led the conversation to the insistent topic of Neaera Witt. George could not help letting fall a hint of his approaching victory.

"Poor woman!" said Mrs. Pocklington. "But, for your sake, I'm very glad."

"Yes, it gets me out of an awkward position."

"Just what my husband said. He thought that you were absolutely bound to prove what you said, or at least to give a good excuse for it."

"Absolutely bound?"

"Well, I mean if you were to keep your place in society."

"And in your house?"

"Oh, he did not go so far as that. Everybody comes to my house."

"Yes; but, Mrs. Pocklington, I don't want to come in the capacity of 'everybody.'"

"Then, I think he did mean that you must do what I say, before you went on coming in any other capacity."

George looked at Mrs. Pocklington. Mrs. Pocklington smiled diplomatically.

"Is Miss Pocklington out?" asked George.

"Yes," said Mrs. Pocklington, "she is out."

"Not back soon?" asked George, smiling in his turn.

"Not yet."

"Not until——?"

"Well, Mr. Neston, I dare say you know what I mean."

"I think so. Fortunately, there is no difficulty. Shall we say Tuesday?"

"When Tuesday comes, we will see if we say Tuesday."

"And, otherwise, I am——?"

- 84 -

"Otherwise, my dear George, you have no one to persuade except——"

"Ah, that is the most difficult task of all."

"I don't know anything about that. Only I hope you believe what you say. Young men are so conceited nowadays."

"When Miss Pocklington comes in, you will tell her how sorry I was not to see her?"

"Certainly."

"And that I look forward to Tuesday?"

"No; I shall say nothing about that. You are not out of the wood yet."

"Oh yes, I am."

But Mrs. Pocklington stood firm; and George departed, feeling that the last possibility of mercy for Neaera Witt had vanished. There is a limit to unselfishness; nay, what place is there for pity when public duty and private interest unite in demanding just severity?

CHAPTER XIV.
NEAERA'S LAST CARD.

NEAERA WITT had one last card to play. Alas, how great the stake, and how slight the chance! Still she would play it. If it failed, she would only drink a little deeper of humiliation, and be trampled a little more contemptuously under foot. What did that matter?

"You will not condemn a woman unheard," she wrote, with a touch of melodrama. "I expect you here on Sunday evening at nine. You cannot be so hard as not to come."

George had written that he would come, but that his determination was unchangeable. "I must come, as you ask me," he said; "but it is useless—worse than useless." Still he would come.

Bill Sykes likes to be tried in a black coat, and draggle-tailed Sal smooths her tangled locks before she enters the dock. Who can doubt, though it be not recorded, that the burghers of Calais, cruelly restricted to their shirts, donned their finest linen to face King Edward and his Queen, or that the Inquisitors were privileged to behold many a robe born to triumph on a different stage? And so Neaera Witt adorned herself to meet George Neston with subtle simplicity. Her own ill-chastened taste, fed upon popular engravings, hankered after black velvet, plainly made in clinging folds; but she fancied that the motive would be too obvious for an eye so *rusé* as George's, and reluctantly surrendered her picture of a second Queen of Scots. White would be better; white could cling as well as black, and would so mingle suggestions of remorse and innocence that surely he could not be hard-hearted enough to draw the distinction. A knot of flowers, destined to be plucked to pieces by agitated hands—so much conventional emotion she could not deny herself,—a dress cut low, and open sleeves made to fall back when the white arms were upstretched for pity,—all this should make a combined assault on George's higher nature and on his lower. Neaera thought that, if only she had been granted time and money to dress properly, she might never have seen the inside of Peckton gaol at all; for even lawyers are human, or, if that be disputed, let us say not superhuman.

George came in with all the awkwardness of an Englishman who hates a scene and feels himself a fool for his awkwardness. Neaera motioned him to a chair, and they sat silent for a moment.

"You sent for me, Mrs. Witt?"

"Yes," said Neaera, looking at the fire. Then, with a sudden turn of her eyes upon him, she added, "It was only—to thank you."

"I'm afraid you have little enough to thank me for."

"Yes; your kindness at Liverpool."

"Oh, it seemed the best way out. I hope you pardon the liberty I took?"

"And for an earlier kindness of yours."

"I really——"

"Yes, yes. When they gave me that money you sent, I cried. I could not cry in prison, but I cried then. It was the first time any one had ever been kind to me."

George was embarrassed. He had an uneasy feeling that the sentiment was trite; but, then, many of the saddest things are the tritest.

"It is good of you," he said, stumbling in his words, "to remember it, in face of all I have done against you."

"You pitied me then."

"With all my heart."

"How did I do it? How did I? I wish I had starved; and seen my father starve first!"

George wondered whether it was food that the late Mr. Gale so urgently needed.

"But I did it. I was a thief; and once a thief, always a thief." And Neaera smiled a sad smile.

"You must not suppose," he said, as he had once before, "that I do not make allowances."

"Allowances?" she cried, starting up. "Allowances—always allowances! never pity! never mercy! never forgetfulness!"

"You did not ask for mercy," said George.

"No, I didn't. I know what you mean—I lied."

"Yes, you lied, if you choose that word. You garbled documents, and, when the truth was told, you called it slander."

Neaera had sunk back in her seat again. "Yes," she moaned. "I couldn't let it all go—I couldn't!"

"You yourself have made pity impossible."

"Oh no, not impossible! I loved him so, and he—he was so trustful."

"The more reason for not deceiving him," said George, grimly.

"What is it, after all?" she exclaimed, changing her tone. "What is it, I say?"

"Well, if you ask me, Mrs. Witt, it's an awkward record."

"An awkward record! Yes, but for a man in love?"

"That's Gerald's look-out. He can do as he pleases."

"What, after you have put me to open shame? And for what? Because I loved my father most, and loved my—the man who loved me—most!" George shook his head.

"If you were in love—in love, I say, with a girl—yes, if you were in love with me, would this thing stop you?" And she stood before him proudly and scornfully.

George looked at her. "I don't think it would," he said.

"Then," she asked, advancing a step, and stretching out her clasped hands, "why ask more for another than for yourself?"

"Gerald will be the head of the family, to begin with——"

"The family?"

"Certainly; the Neston family."

"Who are they? Are they famous? I never heard of them till the other day."

"I daresay not; we moved in rather different circles."

"Do you take pleasure in being brutal?"

"I take pleasure in nothing connected with this confounded affair," said George, impatiently.

"Then why not drop it?"

George shook his head.

"Too late," he said.

"It's mere selfishness. You are only thinking of what people will say of you."

"I have a right to consider that."

"It's mean—mean and heartless!"

George rose. "Really, it's no use going on with this," said he. And, making a slight bow, he turned towards the door.

"I didn't mean it—I didn't mean it," cried Neaera. "But I am out of my mind. Ah, have pity on me!" And she flung herself on the floor, right in his path.

George felt very absurd. He stood, his hat in one hand, his stick and gloves in the other, while Neaera clasped his legs below the knee, and, he feared, was about to bedew his boots with her tears.

"This is tragedy, I suppose," he thought. "How the devil am I to get away?"

"I have never had a chance," Neaera went on, "never. Ah, it is hard! And when at last——" Her voice choked, and George, to his horror, heard her sob.

He nervously shifted his feet about, as well as Neaera's eager clutches would allow him. How he wished he had not come!

"I cannot bear it!" she cried. "They will all write about me, and jeer at me; and Gerald will cast me off. Where shall I hide?—where shall I hide? What was it to you?"

Then she was silent, but George heard her stifled weeping. Her clasp relaxed, and she fell forward, with her face on the floor, in front of him. He did not seize his chance of escape.

"London is uninhabitable to me, if I do as you ask," he said.

She looked up, the tears escaping from her eyes.

"Ah, and the world to me, if you don't!"

George sat down in an arm-chair; he abandoned the hope of running away. Neaera rose, pushed back her hair from her face, and fixed her eyes eagerly on him. He looked down for an instant, and she shot a hasty glance at the mirror, and then concentrated her gaze on him again, a little anxious smile coming to her lips.

"You will?" she asked in a whisper.

George petulantly threw his gloves on a table near him. Neaera advanced, and knelt down beside him, laying her hand on his shoulder.

"You have made me cry so much," she said. "See, my eyes are dim. You won't make me cry any more?"

George looked at the bright eyes, half veiled in tears, and the mouth trembling on the brink of fresh weeping. And the eyes and mouth were very good.

"It is Gerald," she said; "he is so strict. And the shame, the shame!"

"You don't know what it means to me."

"I do indeed: I know it is hard. But you are generous. No, no, don't turn your face away!"

George still sat silent. Neaera took his hand in hers.

"Ah, do!" she said.

George smiled,—at himself, not at Neaera.

"Well, don't cry any more," said he, "or the eyes will be red as well as dim."

"You will, you will?" she whispered eagerly.

He nodded.

"Ah, you are good! God bless you, George: you are good!"

"No. I am only weak."

Neaera swiftly bent and kissed his hand. "The hand that gives me life," she said.

"Nonsense," said George, rather roughly.

"Will you clear me altogether?"

"Oh yes; everything or nothing,"

"Will you give me that—that character?"

"Yes."

She seized his reluctant hand, and kissed it again.

"I have your word?"

"You have."

She leapt up, suddenly radiant.

"Ah, George, Cousin George, how I love you! Where is it?"

George took the document out of his pocket.

Neaera seized it. "Light a candle," she cried.

George with an amused smile obeyed her.

"You hold the candle, and I will burn it!" And she watched the paper consumed with the look of a gleeful child. Then she suddenly stretched her arms. "Oh, I am tired!"

"Poor child!" said George. "You can leave it to me now."

"However shall I repay you? I never can." Then she suddenly saw the cat, ran to him, and picked him up. "We are forgiven, Bob! we are forgiven!" she cried, dancing about the room.

George watched her with amusement.

She put the cat down and came to him. "See, you have made me happy. Is that enough?"

"It is something," said he.

"And here is something more!" And she threw her arms round his neck, and kissed him.

"That's better," said George. "Any more?"

"Not till we are cousins."

"Be gentle in your triumph."

"No, no; don't talk like that. Are you going?"

"Yes. I must go and put things straight."

"Good-bye. I—I hope you won't find it very hard."

"I have been paid in advance."

Neaera blushed a little.

"You shall be better paid, if ever I can," she said.

George paused outside, to light a cigarette; then he struck into the park, and walked slowly along, meditating as he went. When he arrived at Hyde Park Corner, he roused himself from his reverie.

"Now the woman was very fair!" said he, as he hailed a hansom.

CHAPTER XV.
A LETTER FOR MR. GERALD.

MRS. POCKLINGTON sat with blank amazement in her face, and a copy of the second edition of the *Bull's-eye* in her hand. On the middle page, in type widely spaced, beneath a noble headline, appeared a letter from George Neston, running thus:—

"To the Editor of the *Bull's-eye*.

"SIR,

"As you have been good enough to interest yourself, and, I hope, fortunate enough to interest your readers, in the subject of certain allegations made by me in respect of a lady whose name has been mentioned in your columns, I have the honour to inform you that such allegations were entirely baseless, the result of a chance resemblance between that lady and another person, and of my own hasty conclusions drawn therefrom. I have withdrawn all my assertions, fully and unreservedly, and have addressed apologies for them to those who had a right to receive apologies.

"I have the honour to be, sir,
"Your obedient servant,
"GEORGE NESTON."

And then a column of exultation, satire, ridicule, preaching, praying, prophesying, moralising, and what not. The pen flew with wings of joy, and ink was nothing regarded on that day.

Mrs. Pocklington was a kind-hearted woman; yet, when she read a sister's vindication, she found nothing better to say than—

"How very provoking!"

And it may be that this unregenerate exclamation fairly summed up public feeling, if only public feeling had been indecent enough to show itself openly. A man shown to be a fool is altogether too common a spectacle; a woman of fashion proved a thief would have been a more piquant dish. But in this world—and, indeed, probably in any other—we must take what we can get; and since society could not trample on Neaera Witt, it consoled itself by correcting and chastening the misguided spirit of George Neston. Tommy Myles shook his empty little head, and all the other empty heads shook solemnly in time. Isabel Bourne said she knew she was right, and Sidmouth Vane thought there must be something behind—he always did, as became a statesman in the raw. Mr. Espion re-echoed his own leaders, like a phonograph; and the chairman of the Themis thanked Heaven they were out of an awkward job.

But wrath and fury raged in the breast of Laura Pocklington. She thought George had made a fool of her. He had persuaded her to come over to his side, and had then betrayed the colours. There would be joy in Gath and Askelon; or, in other words, Isabel Bourne and Maud Neston would crow over her insupportably.

"I will never see him or speak to him again, mamma," Laura declared, passionately. "He has behaved abominably!"

This announcement rather took the wind out of Mrs. Pocklington's sails. She was just preparing to bear majestically down upon her daughter with a stern *ultimatum* to the effect that, for the present, George must be kept at a distance, and daughters must be guided by their mothers. At certain moments nothing is more annoying than to meet with agreement, when one intends to extort submission.

"Good gracious, Laura!" said Mrs. Pocklington, "you can't care much for the man."

"Care for him! I detest him!"

"My dear, it hardly looked like it."

"You must allow me some self-respect, mamma."

Mr. Pocklington, entering, overheard these words. "Hallo!" said he. "What's the matter?"

"Why, my dear, Laura declares that she will have nothing to say to George Neston."

"Well, that's just your own view, isn't it?" A silence ensued. "It seems to me you are agreed."

It really did look like it; but they had been on the verge of a pretty quarrel all the same: and Mr. Pocklington was confirmed in the opinion he had lately begun to entertain that, when paradoxes of mental process are in question, there is in truth not much to choose between wives and daughters.

Meanwhile, George Neston was steadily and unflinchingly devouring his humble-pie. He sought and obtained Gerald's forgiveness, after half an hour of grovelling abasement. He listened to Tommy Myles's grave rebuke and Sidmouth Vane's cynical raillery without a smile or a tear. He even brought himself to accept with docility a letter full of Christian feeling which Isabel Bourne was moved to write.

All these things, in fact, affected him little in comparison with the great question of his relations with the Pocklingtons. That, he felt, must be settled at once, and, with his white sheet yet round him and his taper still in his hand, he went to call on Mrs. Pocklington.

He found that lady in an attitude of aggressive tranquillity. With careful ostentation she washed her hands of the whole affair. Left to her own way, she might have been inclined to consider that George's foolish recklessness had been atoned for by his manly retractation—or, on the other hand, she might not. It mattered very little which would have been the case; and, if it comforted him, he was at liberty to suppose that she would have embraced the former opinion. The decision did not lie with her. Let him ask Laura and Laura's father. They had made up their minds, and it was not in her province or power to try to change their minds for them. In fact, Mrs. Pocklington took up the position which Mr. Spenlow has made famous—only she had two partners where Mr. Spenlow had but one. George had a shrewd idea that her neutrality covered a favourable inclination towards himself, and thanked her warmly for not ranking herself among his enemies.

"I am even emboldened," he said, "to ask your advice how I can best overcome Miss Pocklington's adverse opinion."

"Laura thinks you have made her look foolish. You see, she took your cause up rather warmly."

"I know. She was most generous."

"You were so very confident."

"Yes; but one little thing at the end tripped me up. I couldn't have foreseen it. Mrs. Pocklington, do you think she will be very obdurate?"

"Oh, I've nothing to do with it. Don't ask me."

"I wish I could rely on your influence."

"I haven't any influence," declared Mrs. Pocklington. "She's as obstinate as a—as resolute as her father."

George rose to go. He was rather disheartened; the price he had to pay for the luxury of generosity seemed very high.

Mrs. Pocklington was moved to pity. "George," she said, "I feel like a traitor, but I will give you one little bit of advice."

"Ah!" cried George, his face brightening. "What is it, my dear Mrs. Pocklington?"

"As to my husband, I say nothing; but as to Laura——"

"Yes, yes!"

"Let her alone—absolutely."

"Let her alone! But that's giving it up."

"Don't call, don't write, don't be known to speak of her. There, I've done what I oughtn't; but you're an old friend of mine, George."

"But I say, Mrs. Pocklington, won't some other fellow seize the chance?"

"If she likes you best, what does that matter? If she doesn't——" And Mrs. Pocklington shrugged her shoulders.

George was convinced by this logic. "I will try," he said.

"Try?"

"Yes, try to let her alone. But it's difficult."

"Stuff and nonsense. Laura isn't indispensable."

"I know those are not your real views."

"You're not her mother; for which you may thank Heaven."

"I do," said George, and took his leave, rather consoled. He would have been even more cheerful had he known that Laura's door was ajar, and Laura was listening for the bang of the hall door. When she heard it, she went down to her mother.

"Who was your visitor, mamma?"

"Oh, George Neston."

"What did *he* come about?"

"Well, my dear, to see me, I suppose."

"And what did he find to say for himself?"

"Oh, we hardly talked about that affair at all. However, he seems in very good spirits."

"I'm sure he has no business to be."

"Perhaps not, my dear; but he was."

"I didn't know it was Mr. Neston. I'm so glad I didn't come down."

Mrs. Pocklington went on knitting.

"I expect he knew why,"

Mrs. Pocklington counted three pearl and three plain.

"Did he say anything about it, mamma?"

"One, two, three. About what, dear?"

"Why, about—about my not coming?"

"No. I suppose he thought you were out."

"Did you tell him so?"

"He didn't ask, my dear. He has other things to think about than being attentive to young women."

"It's very lucky he has," said Laura, haughtily.

"My dear, he lets you alone. Why can't you let him alone?"

Laura took up a book, and Mrs. Pocklington counted her stitches in a brisk and cheerful tone.

It will be seen that George had a good friend in Mrs. Pocklington. In truth he needed some kindly countenance, for society at large had gone mad in praise of Neaera and Gerald. They were the fashion. Everybody tried to talk to them; everybody was coming to the wedding; everybody raved about Neaera's sweet patience and Gerald's unwavering faith. When Neaera drove her lover round the park in her victoria, their journey was a triumphal progress; and only the burden of preparing for the wedding prevented the pair being honoured guests at every select gathering. Gerald walked on air. His open hopes were realised, his secret fears laid to rest; while Neaera's exaggerated excuses for George betrayed to his eyes nothing but the exceeding sweetness of her disposition. Her absolute innocence explained and justified her utter absence of resentment, and must, Gerald felt, add fresh pangs to George's remorse and shame. These pangs Gerald did not feel it his duty to mitigate.

Thursday came, and Monday was the wedding-day. The atmosphere was thick with new clothes, cards of invitation, presents, and congratulations. A thorny question had arisen as to whether George should be invited. Neaera's decision was in his favour, and Gerald himself had written the note, hoping all the while that his cousin's own good sense would keep him away.

"It would be hardly decent in him to come," he said to his father.

"I daresay he will make some excuse," answered Lord Tottlebury. "But I hope you won't keep up the quarrel."

"Keep up the quarrel! By Jove, father, I'm too happy to quarrel."

"Gerald," said Maud Neston, entering, "here's such a funny letter for you! I wonder it ever reached."

She held out a dirty envelope, and read the address—

"Mr. Nesston, Esq.,
"His Lordship Tottilberry,
"London."

"Who in the world is it?" asked Maud, laughing.

Gerald had no secrets.

"I don't know," said he. "Give it me, and we'll see." He opened the letter. The first thing he came upon was a piece of tissue paper neatly folded. Opening it, he found it to be a ten-pound note. "Hullo! is this a wedding present?" said he with a laugh.

"Ten pounds! How funny!" exclaimed Maud. "Is there no letter?"

"Yes, here's a letter!" And Gerald read it to himself.

The letter ran as follows, saving certain eccentricities of spelling which need not be reproduced:—

"SIR,

"I don't rightly know whether this here is your money or Nery's. Nor I don't know *where it comes from*, after what you said when you was here with her Friday. I can work for my living, thanks be to Him to whom thanks is due, and I don't put money in my pocket as I don't know whose pocket it come out of.

"Your humble servant,
"SUSAN BORT."

"Susan Bort!" exclaimed Gerald. "Now, who the deuce is Susan Bort, and what the deuce does she mean?"

"Unless you tell us what she says——" began Lord Tottlebury.

Gerald read the letter again, with a growing feeling of uneasiness. He noticed that the postmark was Liverpool. It so chanced that he had not been to Liverpool for more than a year. And who was Susan Bort?

He got up, and, making an apology for not reading out his letter, went to his own room to consider the matter.

"'Nery?'" said he. "And if I wasn't there, who was?"

It was generous of George Neston to shield Neaera at Liverpool. It was also generous of Neaera to send Mrs. Bort ten pounds immediately after that lady had treated her so cruelly. It was honest of Mrs. Bort to refuse to accept money which she thought might be the proceeds of burglary. To these commendable actions Gerald was indebted for the communication which disturbed his bliss.

"I wonder if Neaera can throw any light on it," said Gerald. "It's very queer. After lunch, I'll go and see her."

CHAPTER XVI.
THERE IS AN EXPLOSION.

MR. BLODWELL was entertaining Lord Mapledurham at luncheon at the Themis Club. The Marquis was not in an agreeable mood. He was ill, and when he was ill he was apt to be cross. His host's calm satisfaction with the issue of the Neston affair irritated him.

"Really, Blodwell," he said, "I sometimes think a lawyer's wig is like Samson's hair. When he takes it off, he takes off all his wits with it. Your simplicity is positively childish."

Mr. Blodwell gurgled contentedly over a basin of soup.

"I think no evil unless I'm paid for it," he said, wiping his mouth. "George found he was wrong, and said so."

"I saw the girl in the Park yesterday," the Marquis remarked. "She's a pretty girl."

"Uncommonly. But I'm not aware that being pretty makes a girl a thief."

"No, but it makes a man a fool."

"My dear Mapledurham!"

"Did he ever tell you what he found out at Liverpool?"

"Did he go to Liverpool?"

"Did he go? God bless the man! Of course he went, to look for——"

Lord Mapledurham stopped, to see who was throwing a shadow over his plate.

"May I join you?" asked Sidmouth Vane, who thought he was conferring a privilege. "I'm interested in what you are discussing."

"Oh, it's you, is it? Have you been listening?"

"No, but everybody's discussing it. Now, I agree with you, Lord Mapledurham. It's a put-up job."

"I expect you thought it was a put-up job when they baptised you, didn't you?" inquired the Marquis.

"And looked for poison in your bottle?" added Blodwell.

Vane gently waved his hand, as if to scatter these clumsy sarcasms. "A man may not be sixty and yet not be an ass," he languidly observed. "Waiter, some salmon, and a pint of 44."

"And may be sixty and yet be an ass, eh?" said the Marquis, chuckling.

"Among ourselves, why do you suppose he let her off?" asked Vane.

The Marquis pushed back his chair. "My young friend, you are too wise. Something will happen to you."

"Hallo!" exclaimed Vane, "here's Gerald Neston."

Gerald came hastily up to Mr. Blodwell. "Do you know where George is?" he asked.

"I believe he's in the club somewhere," answered Mr. Blodwell.

"No, he isn't. I want to see him on business."

Lord Mapledurham rose. "I know your father, Mr. Neston," he said. "You must allow me to shake hands with you, and congratulate you on your approaching marriage."

Gerald received his congratulations with an absent air. "I must go and find George," he said, and went out.

"There!" said Vane, triumphantly. "Don't you see there's something up now?"

The elder men tried to snub him, but they glanced at one another and silently admitted that it looked as if he were right.

Mrs. Bort's letter had stirred into activity all the doubts that Gerald Neston had tried to stifle, and had at last succeeded in silencing. There was a darkly mysterious tone about the document that roused his suspicions. Either there was a new and a more unscrupulous plot against his bride, or else—— Gerald did not finish his train of thought, but he determined to see Neaera at once, as George could not be found without a journey to the Temple, and a journey to the Temple was twice as far as a journey to Albert Mansions. Nevertheless, had Gerald known what was happening at the Temple, he would have gone there first; for in George's chambers, at that very moment, George was sitting in his chair, gazing blankly at Neaera Witt, who was walking restlessly up and down.

"You sent her ten pounds?" he gasped.

"Yes, yes," said Neaera. "I can't let the creature starve."

"But why in the world did she send it back to Gerald?"

"Oh, can't you see? Why, you said you were Gerald; at least, it came to that."

"And she meant to send it to me?"

"Yes, but I had told her my Mr. Neston was Lord Tottlebury's son; so I suppose the letter has gone to Gerald. It must have, if you haven't got it."

"But why should she send it to either of us?"

"Oh, because I said I sent it with Mr. Neston's approval."

"That wasn't true."

"Of course not. But it sounded better."

"Ah, it's dangerous work."

"I should never have done it, if I had foreseen this."

George knew that this represented Neaera's extreme achievement in penitence, and did not press the question.

"What a wretch the woman is," Neaera continued. "Oh, what is to be done? Gerald is sure to ask for an explanation."

"Quite possible, I should think."

"Well, then, I am lost."

"You'd better tell him all about it."

"I can't; indeed I can't. You won't, will you? Oh, you will stand by me?"

"I don't know what Mrs. Bort has said, and so——"

He was interrupted by a knock at the door. George rose and opened it. "What is it, Timms?"

"Mr. Gerald, sir, wants to see you on important business."

"Is he in his room?"

"Yes, sir. I told him you were engaged."

"You didn't tell him Mrs. Witt was here?"

"No, sir."

"Say I'll be with him in a few minutes."

George shut the door, and said, "Gerald's here, and wants to see me."

"Gerald! Then he has got the letter!"

"What do you propose to do, Mrs. Witt?"

"How can I tell? I don't know what she said. She only told me she had sent back the money, and told him why."

"If she told him why——"

"I'm ruined," said Neaera, wringing her hands.

George stood with his back to the fireplace, and regarded her critically. After a moment's pause, he said, with a smile,

"I knew it all—and you were not ruined."

"Ah, you are so good!"

"Nonsense," said George, with a broader smile.

Neaera looked up at him, and smiled too.

"Mightn't you risk it? Of course, truth is dangerous, but he's very fond of you."

"Won't you help me?"

A heavy step and the sound of impatient pushing of furniture were heard from the next room.

"Gerald is getting tired of waiting," said George.

"Won't you do anything?" asked Neaera again, barely repressing a sob.

"Supposing I were willing to lie, where is a possible lie? How can I explain it?"

Timms knocked and entered. Gerald begged for a minute's interview, on pressing business.

"In a moment," said George. Then, turning to Neaera, he added brusquely, "Come, you must decide, Mrs. Witt."

Neaera was no longer in a condition to decide anything. Tears were her ready refuge in time of trouble, and she was picturesquely weeping—for she possessed that rare gift—in the old leathern arm-chair.

"Will you leave it to me?" asked George. "I'll do the best I can."

Neaera sobbed forth the opinion that George was her only friend.

"I shall tell him everything," said George. "Do you authorise me to do that?"

"Oh, how miserable I am!—oh, yes, yes."

"Then stop crying, and try to look nice."

"Why?"

"Because I shall bring him in."

"Oh!" cried Neaera in dismay. But when George went out, she made her hair a little rougher—for so paradoxically do ladies set about the task of ordering their appearance—and anointed her eyes with the contents of a mysterious phial, produced from a recondite pocket. Then she sat up straight, and strained her ears to catch any sound from the next room, where her fate was being decided. She could distinguish which of the two men was speaking, but not the words. First Gerald, then George, then Gerald again. Next, for full five minutes, George talked in low but seemingly emphatic tones. Then came a sudden shout from Gerald.

"Here!" he cried. "In your room!"

They had risen, and were moving about. Neaera's heart beat, though she sat still as a statue. The door was flung open, and she rose to meet Gerald, as he entered with a rush. George followed, with a look of mingled anger and perplexity on his face. Gerald flung a piece of paper at Neaera; it was Mrs. Bort's letter, and, as it fell at her feet, she sank back again in her chair, with a bitter little cry. The worst had happened.

"Thank God for an honest woman!" cried Gerald.

"Gerald!" she murmured, stretching out her hands to him.

"Ah, you can do that to him!" he answered, pointing to George.

"I—I loved you," she said.

"He'll believe you, perhaps—or help you in your lies. I've done with you."

He passed his hand over his brow, and went on. "I was easy to hoodwink, wasn't I? Only a little wheedling and fondling—only a kiss or two—and a lie or two! I believed it all. And you," he added, turning on George, "you spared her, you pitied her, you sacrificed yourself. A fine sacrifice!"

George put his hands in his pockets, and shrugged his shoulders.

"I shouldn't go on before Mrs. Witt," he remarked.

"Not go on! No, no. She's so pure, so innocent, isn't she? Worth any sacrifice?"

"What do you mean, Gerald?" said Neaera.

"You don't know?" he asked, with a sneer. "What does a man ask for what he's done? and what will a woman give? Will give? Has given?"

"Hold your tongue!" said George, laying a hand on his shoulder.

Neaera sat still, gazing at her lover with open eyes: only a little shudder ran over her.

"You duped me nicely between you," Gerald continued, "me and all the world. No truth in it all! A mistake!—all a mistake! He found out—his mistake!" His voice rose almost to a shriek, and ended in a bitter laugh.

"You needn't be a brute," said George, coldly.

Gerald looked at him, then at Neaera, and uttered another sneering laugh. George was close by him now, seeming to watch every motion of his lips. Neaera rose from her chair, and flung herself at the feet of the angry man.

"Ah, Gerald, my love, have pity!" she wailed.

"Pity!" he echoed, drawing back, so that she fell on her face before him. "Pity! I might pity a thief, I might pity a liar, I have no pity for a——"

The sentence went unfinished, for, with a sudden motion, George closed on him, and flung him through the open door out of the room.

"Finish your blackguardism outside!" he said, as he shut the door and turned the key.

CHAPTER XVII.
LAURA DIFFERS.

IRA brevis furor, says the moralist; and the adjective is the only part of the saw that is open to exception. Gerald Neston's wrath burnt fiercely, but it burnt steadily also, and reflection brought with it nothing but a stronger conviction of his wrongs. To George, the interpretation his cousin put on his action in shielding Neaera seemed to argue that uncommon degree of wrong-headedness that is hardly distinguishable from immorality. Yet, in the recesses of George's heart lurked the knowledge that Mrs. Witt, plain, old, unattractive, might have reaped scant mercy, at his hands; and Gerald, if he did not believe all he had brutally hinted, believed quite enough of it to make him regard George as a traitor and Neaera as an intriguer. What sane man could have acted as George had acted, unless under a woman's fascination? Jealousy did the rest, for Neaera herself had sapped the strength of her lover's trust in her, and he doubted not that she who had deluded him in everything else had not hesitated to practise on him the last deceit. She and George were confederates. Need any one ask how they became so, or what the terms of the alliance were?

It was hardly wonderful that this theory, strange as it seemed, should find a place in Gerald's disordered mind, or that, having done so, it should vent itself in intemperate words and reckless sneers. It was, however, more remarkable that the opinion gained some general favour. It pleased the cynical, for it explained away what seemed like a generous action; it pleased the gossips, for it introduced into the Neston affair the topic most congenial to gossips; it pleased the "unco guid," for it pointed the moral of the ubiquity of sin; it pleased men as a sex, because it made George's conduct natural and explicable; it pleased women as a sex, because it ratified the opinion they had always held of beautiful mysterious widows in general, and of Neaera Witt in particular. And amid this chorus, the voice of the charitable, admitting indiscretion, but asserting generosity, was lost and hushed, and George's little band of friends and believers were dubbed blind partisans and, by consequence, almost accomplices.

Fortunately for George, among his friends were men who cared little for public reprobation. Mr. Blodwell did his work, ate his dinner, said what he thought, and esteemed the opinion of society much at the value the Duke of Wellington set upon the views of the French nation. As for Lord Mapledurham and Sidmouth Vane, unpopularity was the breath of their nostrils; and Vane did not hesitate to purchase the pleasure of being in a minority by a sacrifice of consistency; he abandoned the theory which he had been among the first to suggest, as soon as the suggestion passed by general acceptance into vulgarity.

The three men gave George Neston a dinner, drank Neaera's health, and allowed themselves an attitude of almost contemptuous protest against the verdict of society—a verdict forcibly expressed by the *Bull's-eye*, when it declared with not unnatural warmth that it had had enough of this "sordid affair." But then the *Bull's-eye* had hardly shown its wonted perspicacity, and Mr. Espion declared that he had not been treated in a respectful way. There was no traversing the fact; George's party fell back on a denial of the obligation.

Mankind is so constructed that the approbation of man does not satisfy man, nor that of woman woman. If all the clubs had been ringing with his praises, George Neston would still have turned his first and most eager glance to Mrs. Pocklington's. As it was, he thought of little else than what view of his conduct would gain the victory there. Alas! he knew only too soon. Twice he called: twice was entrance refused him. Then came a note from Mrs. Pocklington—an unanswerable note; for the lady asserted nothing and denied nothing; she intrenched herself behind common opinion. She, as George knew, was a tolerably independent person so far as her own fame was concerned: but where her daughter was interested, it was another thing; Laura's suitor must not be under a cloud; Laura's future must not be jeopardied; Laura's affections must be reposed only where absolute security could be guaranteed. Mr. Pocklington agreed with his wife to the full. Hence there must be an end of everything—so far as the Pocklington household was concerned, an end of George Neston. And poor George read the decree, and groaned in his heart. Nevertheless, strange events were happening behind that door, so firmly, so impenetrably closed to George's eager feet— events to Mrs. Pocklington inconceivable, even while they actually happened; to her husband, alarming, reprehensible, extraordinary, puzzling, amusing, almost, in a way, delightful. In fine, Laura rebelled. And the declaration of independence was promulgated on this wise.

Mrs. Pocklington had conveyed to her daughter, with all delicacy requisite and imaginable, the new phase of the affair. It shocked and distressed her to allude to such things; but Laura was a woman now, and must know—and so forth. And Laura heard it all with no apparent shock—nay, with a calmness approaching levity; and when she was told that all communications between herself and George must cease, she shook her pretty head and retired to her bedroom, neither accepting nor protesting against the decision.

The next morning after breakfast she appeared, equipped for a walk, holding a letter in her hand. Mrs. Pocklington had ordered her household, and had now sat down to a comfortable hour with a novel before luncheon. *Dis aliter visum.*

"I am going out, mamma," Laura began, "to post this note to Mr. Neston."

Mrs. Pocklington never made mistakes in the etiquette of names, and assumed a like correctness in others. She imagined her daughter referred to Gerald. "Why need you write to him?" she asked, looking up. "He's nothing more than an acquaintance."

"Mamma! He's an intimate friend."

"Gerald Neston an intimate friend! Why——"

"I mean Mr. George Neston," said Laura, in a calm voice, but with a slight blush.

"George!" exclaimed Mrs. Pocklington. "What in the world do you want to write to George Neston for? I have said all that is necessary."

"I thought I should like to say something too."

"My dear, certainly not. If you had been—if there had been anything actually arranged, perhaps a line from you would have been right; though, under the circumstances, I doubt it. As it is, for you to write would simply be to give him a chance of reopening the acquaintance."

Laura did not sit down, but stood by the door, prodding the carpet with the point of her parasol. "Is the acquaintance closed?" she asked, after a pause.

"You remember, surely, what I said yesterday? I hope it's not necessary to repeat it."

"Oh no, mamma; I remember it." Laura paused, gave the carpet another prod, and went on, "I'm just writing to say I don't believe a word of it."

"Jack's Darling" fell from Mrs. Pocklington's paralysed grasp.

"Laura, how dare you? It is enough for you that I have decided what is to be done."

"You see, mamma, when everybody is turning against him, I want to show him he has one friend, at least, who doesn't believe these hateful stories."

"I wonder you haven't more self-respect. Considering what is said about him and Neaera Witt——"

"Oh, bother Mrs. Witt!" said Laura, actually smiling. "Really, mamma, it's nonsense; he doesn't care that for Neaera Witt!" And she tried to snap her fingers; but, happily for Mrs. Pocklington's nerves, the attempt was a failure.

"I shall not argue with you, Laura. You will obey me, and there is an end of it."

"You told me I was a woman yesterday. If I am, I ought to be allowed to judge for myself. Anyhow, you ought to hear what I have to say."

"Give me that letter, Laura."

"I'm very sorry, mamma; but——"

"Give it to me."

"Very well; I shall have to write another."

"Do you mean to defy me, Laura?"

Laura made no answer.

Mrs. Pocklington opened and read the letter.

"DEAR MR. NESTON," (it ran)—

"I want you to know that I do not believe a single word of what they are saying. I am very sorry for poor Mrs. Witt, and I think you have acted *splendidly*. Isn't it charming weather? Riding in the park in the morning is a positive delight.

"With kindest regards,

"Yours very sincerely,
"LAURA F. POCKLINGTON."

Mrs. Pocklington gasped. The note was little better than an assignation! "I shall show this to your father," she said, and swept out of the room.

Laura sat down and wrote an exact copy of the offending document, addressed it, stamped it, and put it in her pocket. Then, with ostentatious calmness, she took up "Jack's Darling," and appeared to become immersed in it.

Mrs. Pocklington found it hard to make her husband appreciate the situation; indeed, she had scarcely risen to it herself. Everybody talks of heredity in these days: the Pocklingtons, both people of resolute will, had the opportunity of studying its working in their own daughter. The result was fierce anger in Mrs. Pocklington, mingled anger and admiration in her husband, perplexity in both. Laura's position was simple and well defined. By coercion and imprisonment she might, she admitted, be prevented sending her letter and receiving a reply, but by no other means. Appeals to duty were met by appeals to justice; she parried entreaty by counter-entreaty, reproofs by protestations of respect, orders by silence. What was to be done? Laura was too old, and the world was too old, for violent remedies. Intercepting correspondence meant exposure to the household. The revolt was appalling, absurd, unnatural; but it was also, as Mr. Pocklington admitted, "infernally awkward." Laura realised that its awkwardness was her strength, and, having in vain invited actual physical restraint, in its absence walked out and posted her letter.

Then Mrs. Pocklington acted. At a day's notice she broke up her establishment for the season, and carried her daughter off with her. She gave no address save to her husband. Laura was not allowed to know whither she was being taken. She was, as she bitterly said, "spirited away" by the continental mail, and all the communications cut. Only, just as the brougham was starting, when the last box was on, and Mr. Pocklington, having spoken his final word of exhortation, was waving good-bye from the steps, Laura jumped out, crossed the road, and dropped a note into a pillar-box.

"It is only," she remarked, resuming her seat, "to tell Mr. Neston that I can't give him any address at present."

What, asked Mrs. Pocklington of her troubled mind, were you to do with a girl like that?

CHAPTER XVIII.
GEORGE NEARLY GOES TO BRIGHTON.

ONE evening, about a week after what Mr. Espion called the final *esclandre*, Tommy Myles made his appearance in the smoking-room of the Themis. More important matters have ousted the record of Tommy's marriage and blissful honeymoon, and he came back to find that a negligent world had hardly noticed his absence.

"How are you?" said he to Sidmouth Vane.

"How are you?" said Vane, raising his eyes for a moment from *Punch*.

Tommy sat down by him. "I say," he remarked, "this Neston business is rather neat. We read about it in Switzerland."

"Been away?"

"Of course I have—after my wedding, you know."

"Ah! Seen *Punch*?" And Vane handed it to him.

"I had a pretty shrewd idea of how the land lay. So had Bella."

"Bella?"

"Why, my wife."

"Oh, a thousand pardons. I thought you rather backed Mrs. Witt."

"My dear fellow, we wanted her to have fair play. I suppose there's no question of the marriage now?"

"I suppose not."

"What's the fair Mrs. Witt going to do?"

Vane wanted to be let alone, and Tommy worried him. He turned on the little gentleman with some ferocity. "My dear Tommy," he said, "you backed her through thick and thin, and blackguarded George for attacking her."

"Yes, but——"

"Well, whoever was right, you weren't, so hadn't you better say no more about it?" And Mr. Vane rose and walked away.

In fact, he was thoughtful. What would Mrs. Witt do next? And what would George Neston do? Vane knew of cases where the accusation suggests the crime; it seemed not unlikely that if George had to bear the contumely attaching to a connection with Mrs. Witt, he might think it as well to reap the benefit. He might not have sought to win her favour yet, but it was very possible he might do so now. If he didn't—well, some one would. And Mr. Vane considered that he might find it worth his while to be the man. His great relatives would cry aloud in horror; society would be shocked. But a man will endure something for a pretty woman and five thousand a year. Only, what did George Neston mean to do?

It will be seen that Sidmouth Vane did not share Laura Pocklington's conviction that George cared nothing for Mrs. Witt. Of course he had not Laura's reasons: and perhaps some difference between the masculine and feminine ways of looking at such things must be allowed for. As it happened, however, Vane was right—for a moment. After George had been for a second time repulsed from Mrs. Pocklington's doors, finding the support of his friends unsatisfying and yearning for the more impassioned approval that women give, he went the next day to Neaera's, and intruded on the sorrow-laden retirement to which that wronged lady had betaken herself. And Neaera's grief and gratitude, her sorrow and sympathy, her friendship and fury, were all alike and equally delightful to him.

"The meanness of it!" she cried with flashing eyes. "Oh, I would rather die than have a petty soul like that!"

Gerald was, of course, the subject of these strictures, and George was content not to contradict them.

"He evidently," continued Neaera, "simply cannot understand your generosity. It's beyond him!"

"You mustn't rate what you call my generosity too high," said George. "But what are you going to do, Mrs. Witt?"

Neaera spread her hands out with a gesture of despair.

"What am I to do? I am—desolate."

"So am I. We must console one another."

This speech was indiscreet. George recognised it, when Neaera's answering glance reached him.

"That will make them talk worse than ever," she said, smiling. "You ought never to speak to me again, Mr. Neston."

"Oh, we are damned beyond redemption, so we may as well enjoy ourselves."

"No, you mustn't shock your friends still more."

"I have no friends left to shock," replied George, bitterly.

Neaera implored him not to say that, running over the names of such as might be supposed to remain faithful. George shook his head at each name: when the Pocklingtons were mentioned, his shake was big with sombre meaning.

"Well, well," she said with a sigh, "and now what are you going to do?"

"Oh, nothing. I think some of us are going to have a run to Brighton. I shall go, just to get out of this."

"Is Brighton nice now?"

"Nicer than London, anyhow."

"Yes. Mr. Neston——?"

"Yes, Mrs. Witt? Why don't you come too."

"At any rate, you'd—you and your friends—be somebody to speak to, wouldn't you?" said Neaera, resting her chin on her hand and gazing at George.

"Oh yes, you must come. We shall be very jolly."

"Poor us! But perhaps it will console us to mingle our tears."

"Will you come?" asked George.

"I shan't tell you," she said with a laugh. "It must be purely accidental."

"A fortuitous concurrence? Very well. We go to-morrow."

"I don't want to know when you go."

"No. But we do."

Neaera laughed again, and George took his leave, better pleased with the world than when he arrived. A call on a pretty woman often has this effect; sometimes, let us add, to complete our commonplace, just the opposite.

"Why shouldn't I?" he argued to himself. "I don't know why I should get all the blame for nothing. If they think it of me, I may as well do it."

But when George reached his lodgings, he found on the table, side by side with Mr. Blodwell's final letter about the Brighton trip, Laura Pocklington's note. And then—away went Brighton, and Neaera Witt, and the reckless defiance of public opinion, and all the rest of it! And George swore at himself for a heartless, distrustful, worthless person, quite undeserving to receive such a letter from such a lady. And when the second letter came the next morning, he swore again, at himself for his meditated desertion, and by all his gods, that he would be worthy of such favour.

"The child's a trump," he said, "a regular trump! And she shan't be worried by hearing of me hanging about in Mrs. Witt's neighbourhood."

The happy reflections which ensued were appropriate, but hackneyed, being in fact those of a man much in love. It is, however, worth notice that Laura's refusal to think evil had its reward: for if she had suspected George, she would never have shown him her heart in those letters; and, but for those letters, he might have gone to Brighton, and——; whereas what did happen was something quite different.

CHAPTER XIX.
SOME ONE TO SPEAK TO.

BEING a public character, although an object of ambition to many, has its disadvantages. Fame is very pleasant, but we do not want everybody in the hotel to point at us when we come down to dinner. When Neaera went to Brighton—for it is surely unnecessary to say that she intended to go and did go thither—she felt that the fame which had been thrust upon her debarred her from hotels, and she took lodgings of a severely respectable type, facing the sea. There she waited two days, spending her time walking and driving where all the world walks and drives. There were no signs of George, and Neaera felt aggrieved. She sent him a line, and waited two days more. Then she felt she was being treated as badly as possible—unkindly, negligently, faithlessly, disrespectfully. He had asked her to come; the invitation was as plain as could be: without a word, she was thrown over! In great indignation she told her maid to pack up, and, meanwhile, sallied out to see if the waves would perform their traditional duty of soothing a wounded spirit. The task was a hard one; for, whatever Neaera Witt had suffered, neglect at the hands of man was a grief fortune had hitherto spared her.

She forsook the crowded parade, and strolled down by the water's edge. Presently she sat down under the shade of a boat, and surveyed the waters and the future. She felt very lonely. George had seemed inclined to be pleasant but now he had deserted her. She had no one to speak to. What was the use of being pretty and rich? Everything was very hard and she had done no real harm, and was a very, very miserable girl, and—— Under the shade of the boat, Neaera cried a little, choosing the moment when there were no passers-by.

But one who came from behind escaped her vigilance. He saw the gleam of golden hair, and the slim figure, and the little shapely head bowing forward to meet the gloved hands; and he came down the beach, and, standing behind her for a moment, heard a little gurgle of distress.

"I beg your pardon," said he. "Can I help?"

Neaera looked up with a start. The upright figure, bravely resisting a growing weight of years, the iron-grey hair, the hooked nose, and pleasant keen eyes seemed familiar to her. Surely she had seen him in town!

"Why, it's Mrs. Witt!" he said. "We are acquaintances, or we ought to be." And he held out his hand, adding, with a smile, "I am Lord Mapledurham."

"Oh!" said Neaera.

"Yes," said the Marquis. "Now, I know all about it, and it's a burning shame. And, what's more, it's all my fault."

"Your fault?" she said, in surprise.

"However, I warned George Neston to let it alone. But he's a hot-headed fellow."

"I never thought him that."

"He is, though. Well, look at this. He asks Blodwell, and Vane, and me—at least, he didn't ask me, but Blodwell did—to make a party here. We agree. The next moment—hey, presto! he's off at a tangent!"

Neaera could not make up her mind whether Lord Mapledurham was giving this explanation merely to account for his own presence or also for her information.

"The fact is, you see," the Marquis resumed, "his affairs are rather troublesome. He's out of favour with the authorities, you know—Mrs. Pocklington."

"Does he mind about Mrs. Pocklington?"

"He minds about Miss Pocklington, and I suspect——"

"Yes?"

"That she minds about him. I met Pocklington at the club yesterday, and he told me his people had gone abroad. I said it was rather sudden, but Pocklington turned very gruff, and said 'Not at all.' Of course that wasn't true."

"Oh, I hope she will be good to him," said Neaera. "Fancy, if I were the cause——"

"As I said at the beginning," interrupted the Marquis, "I'm the cause."

"You!"

Then he settled himself by her side, and told her how his reminiscence had been the first thing to set George on the track of discovery, whence all the trouble had resulted.

"So you see," he ended, "you have to put all your woes down to my chatter."

"How strange!" she said, dreamily, looking out to sea.

The Marquis nodded, his eyes scanning her face.

Then she turned to him suddenly, and said, "I was very young, you know, and—rather hungry."

"I am a sinner myself," he answered, smiling.

"And—and what I did afterwards, I——"

"I came to make my confession, not to hear yours. How shall I atone for all I have brought on you? What shall I do now?"

"I—I only want some friends, and—and some one to speak to," said Neaera, with a forlorn little sigh.

The Marquis took her hand and kissed it gallantly. "If that is all," said he, smiling, "perhaps we may manage."

"Thanks," said Neaera, putting her handkerchief into her pocket.

"That's right! Blodwell and Vane are here too, and——"

"I don't much care about them; but——"

"Oh, they're all on your side."

"Are they? I needn't see more of them than I like, need I?"

The Marquis was not young, no, nor inexperienced; but, all the same, he was not proof against this flattery. "Perhaps they won't stay long," he said.

"And you?" she asked.

He smiled at her, and, after a moment of innocent seriousness, her lips wavered into an answering smile.

The Marquis, after taking tea with Neaera and satisfying himself that the lady was not planning immediate flight, strolled back to his hotel in a thoughtful mood. He enjoyed a little triumph over Mr. Blodwell and Sidmouth Vane at dinner; but this did not satisfy him. For almost the first time in his life, he felt the need of an adviser and confidant: he was afraid that he was going to make a fool of himself. Mr. Blodwell withdrew after dinner, to grapple with some papers which had pursued him, and the Marquis sat smoking a cigar on a seat with Vane, struggling against the impulse to trust that young man with his thoughts. Vane was placidly happy: the distant, hypothetical relations between himself and Neaera, the like of which his busy idle brain constructed around every attractive marriageable woman he met, had no power to disturb either his soul or his digestion. If it so fell out, it would be well; but he was conscious that the object would wring from him no very active exertions.

"Mrs. Witt expected to find George here, I suppose?" he asked, flicking the ash from his cigar.

"Yes, I think so."

"Anything on there?"

"Nothing at all, my dear fellow," replied the Marquis, with more confidence than he would have shown twelve hours before. "She knows he's mad about little Laura Pocklington."

"I'll call on her to-morrow," said Vane, with his usual air of gracious condescension.

"She's living very quietly," remarked the Marquis.

Vane turned towards him with a smile and almost a wink. "Oho!" he said.

"Be respectful to your elders, you young dog," said the Marquis.

"You make us forget your claims in that respect. You must be more venerable," answered Vane.

After a moment's silent smoking, "Why don't you marry?" asked the Marquis. It is a question which often means that the questioner's own thoughts are trending in that direction.

"I'm waiting for that heiress." Then he added, perhaps out of good nature, "If it comes to that, why don't you?"

"I'm not anxious to have people pointing at me for an old fool."

"Oh, hang people! Besides, you're not old."

"Fifty-six."

"That's nothing nowadays."

"You're laughing!" said the Marquis, suspiciously.

"Upon my honour, no."

The Marquis laughed too, and put his cigar back in his mouth. He took it out again almost at once. "It wouldn't be bad to have a son," he said. "I mean an heir, you know."

"The first step is a wife then, no doubt."

"Most women are so tedious. Still, you understand my feeling?"

"I might in your position. For myself, I hate brats."

"Ah, you will feel it some day."

Vane thought this rather barefaced. "When did it attack you?" he asked with a smile.

"This afternoon," answered the Marquis, gravely.

Vane's cynical humour was tickled by the *dénoûment* this admission suggested. "Gad! I should like to see Gerald Neston's face!" he chuckled, forgetting his own designs in his gratification.

"Of course she's—well, the deuce of a flirt," said the Marquis.

Vane risked a philosophical generalisation. "All nice women are flirts," he said. "That's what you mean when you call them nice."

"Very pretty and attractive, though."

"And the shoes?"

"Damn the shoes!" said the Marquis.

The next morning, Mr. Blodwell and Sidmouth Vane went to London; but the society papers recorded that the Marquis of Mapledurham prolonged his stay at Brighton.

CHAPTER XX.
FATE'S INSTRUMENTS.

SUMMER and autumn came and went. The season died lingeringly and suffered its slow resurrection. Grouse and partridges, autumn scares and vacation speeches, the yield of the crops and the beginning of the session each had their turn of public favour, and the great Neston sensation died away, galvanised now and again into a fitful spasm of life by Mr. Espion's persevering battery. His efforts were in vain. All the cats were out of all the bags, and the interest of the public was satiated. The actors in the drama, returning to town, as most of them did in the winter, found themselves restored to obscurity; their story, once so eagerly dished up as the latest gossip, was now the stale stock of bores, useful only to regale the very young or the very provincial palate.

All at once, there was a revival. A rumour, a piquant rumour, began to be whispered at the clubs. Men again looked at Gerald Neston, wondering if he had heard it, and at George, asking how he would take it. Mr. Blodwell had to protest ignorance twenty times a day, and Sidmouth Vane intrenched himself in the safe seclusion of his official apartment. If it were true, it was magnificent. Who knew?

Mr. Pocklington heard the rumour, but, communing with his own heart, held his tongue. He would not disturb the peace that seemed again to have settled on his house. Laura, having asserted her independence, had allowed the subject to drop; she had been bright, cheerful, and docile, had seen sights, and gone to entertainments, and made herself agreeable; and Mrs. Pocklington hoped, against a secret conviction, that the rebellion was not only sleeping but dead. She could not banish herself from London; so, with outward confidence and inward fear, she brought her daughter home in November, praying that George Neston might not cross her path, praying too, in her kind heart, that time might remove the silent barrier between her and her daughter, against which she fretted in vain.

But certain other people had no idea of leaving the matter to the slow and uncertain hand of time. There was a plot afoot. George was in it, and Sidmouth Vane, and Mr. Blodwell; so was the Marquis, and another, whose present name it would ruin our deep mystery to disclose—if it be guessed, there is no help for it. And just when Laura was growing sad, and a little hurt and angry at hearing nothing from George, she chanced to have a conversation with Sidmouth Vane, and emerged therefrom, laughing, blushing, and riotously happy, though the only visible outcome of the talk was an invitation for her mother and herself to join in the mild entertainment of afternoon tea at Vane's rooms the next day. Now, Sidmouth Vane was very deceitful; he, so to say, appropriated to his own use and credit Laura's blushes and Laura's laughter, and, when the invitation came, innocent Mrs. Pocklington, without committing herself to an approval of Mr. Vane, rejoiced to think it pleased Laura to take tea with any young man other than George Neston, and walked into the trap with gracious urbanity.

Vane received his guests, Mr. Blodwell supporting him. Mrs. Pocklington and her daughter were the first arrivals, and Vane apologised for the lateness of the others.

"Lord Mapledurham is coming," he said, "and he's been very busy lately."

"I thought he was out of town," said Mrs. Pocklington.

"He only came back yesterday."

The door opened, and Vane's servant announced with much pomp, "The Marquis and Marchioness of Mapledurham."

The Marquis advanced straight to Mrs. Pocklington; then he took Neaera's hand, and said, "You have always been good to me, Mrs. Pocklington. I hope you'll be as good to my wife."

It was hushed up as far as possible, but still it leaked out that, on this sole occasion, Mrs. Pocklington was at a loss—was, in fact, if the word be allowable, flabbergasted. Vane maliciously hinted at burnt feathers and other extreme remedies, and there was really no doubt at all that Laura untied her mother's bonnet-strings.

Neaera stood looking on, half proud, half frightened, till Laura ran to her and kissed her, and called her the best friend she had, with much other emotional language.

Then Mrs. Pocklington came round, and took a cup of tea, and, still unconsciously doing just as she was meant to do, drifted into the balcony with the Marquis, and had a long conversation with him. When she came back, she found Vane ordering a fresh pot of tea.

"But we must really be going," she said. "Mustn't we, Laura?" And as she spoke she took her daughter's hand and patted it.

"Do you expect any one else, Vane?" asked Mr. Blodwell.

"Well, I did, but he's very late."

"Where can he have got to?" asked Neaera, smiling.

"Oh, I know where he is," said Vane. "He's—he's only in the next room."

Everybody looked at Mrs. Pocklington and smiled. She looked at them all, and last at her daughter. Laura was smiling too, but her eyes were eager and imploring.

"If he wants any tea, he had better come in," said Mrs. Pocklington.

So the pair of shoes wrought out their work, giving society yet another sensation, making Neaera Witt a great lady, and Laura Pocklington a happy woman, and confirming all Mrs. Bort's darkest views on the immorality of the aristocracy. And the Marquis and George Neston put their heads together, and caused to be fashioned two dainty little shoes in gold and diamonds, and gave them to their wives, as a sign and remembrance of the ways of destiny. And Neaera wears the shoe, and will talk to you quite freely about Peckton Gaol.

The whole affair, however, shocked Lord Tottlebury very deeply, and Gerald Neston is still a bachelor. Whether this fate be a reward for the merits he displayed, or a punishment for the faults he fell into, let each, according to his prejudices or his experience, decide. *Non nostrum est tantas componere lites.*

Milton Keynes UK
Ingram Content Group UK Ltd.
UKHW020239250424
441687UK00004B/278

9 789357 954693